# SAS® Guide to the REPORT Procedure: Reference

## Release 6.11

SAS Institute Inc.
SAS Campus Drive
Cary, NC 27513

The correct bibliographic citation for this manual is as follows: SAS Institute Inc., *SAS® Guide to the REPORT Procedure: Reference, Release 6.11*, Cary, NC: SAS Institute Inc., 1995. 123 pp.

**SAS® Guide to the REPORT Procedure: Reference, Release 6.11**

Copyright © 1995 by SAS Institute Inc., Cary, NC, USA.

ISBN 1-55544-265-X

SAS Institute Inc., SAS Campus Drive, Cary, North Carolina 27513.

1st printing, October 1995

The SAS® System is an integrated system of software providing complete control over data access, management, analysis, and presentation. Base SAS software is the foundation of the SAS System. Products within the SAS System include SAS/ACCESS®, SAS/AF®, SAS/ASSIST®, SAS/CALC®, SAS/CONNECT®, SAS/CPE®, SAS/DMI®, SAS/EIS®, SAS/ENGLISH®, SAS/ETS®, SAS/FSP®, SAS/GRAPH®, SAS/IMAGE®, SAS/IML®, SAS/IMS-DL/I®, SAS/INSIGHT®, SAS/LAB®, SAS/NVISION®, SAS/OR®, SAS/PH-Clinical®, SAS/QC®, SAS/REPLAY-CICS®, SAS/SESSION®, SAS/SHARE®, SAS/SPECTRAVIEW®, SAS/STAT®, SAS/TOOLKIT®, SAS/TRADER®, SAS/TUTOR®, SAS/DB2™, SAS/GEO™, SAS/GIS™, SAS/PH-Kinetics™, SAS/SHARE*NET™, and SAS/SQL-DS™ software. Other SAS Institute products are SYSTEM 2000® Data Management Software, with basic SYSTEM 2000, CREATE™, Multi-User™, QueX™, Screen Writer™, and CICS interface software; InfoTap® software; NeoVisuals® software; JMP®, JMP IN®, JMP Serve®, and JMP *Design*® software; SAS/RTERM® software; and the SAS/C® Compiler and the SAS/CX® Compiler; VisualSpace™ software; and Emulus® software. MultiVendor Architecture™ and MVA™ are trademarks of SAS Institute Inc. SAS Institute also offers SAS Consulting®, SAS Video Productions®, Ambassador Select®, and On-Site Ambassador™ services. *Authorline*®, Books by Users™, The Encore Series™, *JMPer Cable*®, *Observations*®, *SAS Communications*®, *SAS Training*®, *SAS Views*®, the SASware Ballot®, and SelecText™ documentation are published by SAS Institute Inc. The SAS Video Productions logo and the Books by Users SAS Institute's Author Service logo are registered service marks and the Helplus logo and The Encore Series logo are trademarks of SAS Institute Inc. All trademarks above are registered trademarks or trademarks of SAS Institute Inc. in the USA and other countries. ® indicates USA registration.

The Institute is a private company devoted to the support and further development of its software and related services.

Other brand and product names are registered trademarks or trademarks of their respective companies.

# Contents

**Credits  v**

CHAPTER *1*  . . . . . . . . . . .  **What Can I Do with PROC REPORT?  1**
Three Ways to Use PROC REPORT  **1**
Sample Reports  **1**

CHAPTER *2*  . . . . . . . . . . .  **PROC REPORT Concepts  5**
Report Layout  **5**
Compute Blocks  **11**
Break Lines  **14**
Printing a Report  **15**
Storing and Re-Using a Report Definition  **16**
Using Form Characters  **16**

CHAPTER *3*  . . . . . . . . . . .  **Syntax and Examples  19**
Examples  **48**

CHAPTER *4*  . . . . . . . . . . .  **PROC REPORT Windows  77**

CHAPTER *5*  . . . . . . . . . . .  **How PROC REPORT Builds a Report  103**
Introduction  **103**
Sequence of Events  **103**
Building a Report that Uses Groups and a Report Summary  **105**
Building a Report that Uses DATA Step Variables  **109**

**Index  117**

iv

# Credits

## Documentation

| | |
|---|---|
| Design and Production | Design, Production, and Printing Services |
| Style Programming | Publications Technology Development |
| Technical Review | Patricia L. Berryman, Ellen B. Daniels, Alan R. Eaton, Hillary Freeman, Nancy L. Goodling, John E. Green III, Chris Hanson, Donald J. Henderson, Christina A. Hobbs, Martha F. Johnson, Christine C. Kelly, Theresa Lautato, Deborah P. Morrison, Debra Perry, Randall D. Poindexter, Philip R. Shelton, Linda L. Timberlake, Donna L. Torrence, Linda Walters, Ronda Watts |
| Writing and Editing | Joan M. Stout, Helen F. Wolfson |

## Software

| | |
|---|---|
| Applications | Alan R. Eaton |
| Technical Support | John E. Green III, Christina A. Hobbs |

CHAPTER *1* # What Can I Do with PROC REPORT?

*Three Ways to Use PROC REPORT*   **1**
*Sample Reports*   **1**

## Three Ways to Use PROC REPORT

PROC REPORT combines features of PROC PRINT, PROC MEANS, PROC TABULATE, and the DATA step into a single report-writing tool that can produce a variety of reports. You can use PROC REPORT in three ways:

☐ in a windowing environment with a prompting facility that guides you as you build a report.

☐ in a windowing environment without the prompting facility.

☐ in a nonwindowing environment. In this case, you submit a series of statements with the PROC REPORT statement, just as you do in other SAS procedures.

You can submit these statements from the PROGRAM EDITOR window with the NOWINDOWS option in the PROC REPORT statement or run SAS in batch, noninteractive, or interactive line mode (see "Running the System" in Chapter 1 of *SAS Language: Reference*).

This document provides reference information on using PROC REPORT in a windowing or nonwindowing environment. This information is also available online through the HELP system. The HELP system also provides some task-oriented information for the windowing environment (under "How to . . ."). Task-oriented documentation for the nonwindowing environment is in SAS Technical Report P-258, *Using the REPORT Procedure in a Nonwindowing Environment, Release 6.07.*

**Note:**   The FSREPORT command in SAS/FSP software gives you more control over fonts and colors than PROC REPORT does. For information on the FSREPORT command, see *SAS Software: Changes and Enhancements, Release 6.11.*

## Sample Reports

A *detail report* contains one row for every observation selected for the report. Each of these rows is a *detail row*. A *summary report* consolidates data so that each detail row represents multiple observations.

Both detail and summary reports can contain *summary lines* as well as detail rows. A summary line summarizes numerical data for a set of detail rows or for all detail rows. PROC REPORT provides both default and customized summaries (see "Break Lines" on page 14).

The reports in this section give you an idea of the kinds of reports that PROC REPORT can produce. See "Examples" on page 48 for more reports and for the code that creates them.

The data set that these reports use contains one day's sales figures for eight stores in a chain of grocery stores. Each observation contains the day's sales for one department in one store. The store is identified by the sector of the city that it is in and by the name of the manager.

**Unordered detail report with a Default Summary.** In this report, the order of the rows matches the order of the observations in the input data set. Even an unordered detail report can contain summary information for all the rows of the report. This report displays the default summary.

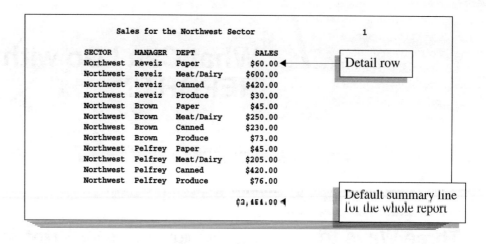

```
                    Sales for the Northwest Sector                        1

        SECTOR      MANAGER   DEPT              SALES
        Northwest   Reveiz    Paper            $60.00
        Northwest   Reveiz    Meat/Dairy      $600.00
        Northwest   Reveiz    Canned          $420.00
        Northwest   Reveiz    Produce          $30.00
        Northwest   Brown     Paper            $45.00
        Northwest   Brown     Meat/Dairy      $250.00
        Northwest   Brown     Canned          $230.00
        Northwest   Brown     Produce          $73.00
        Northwest   Pelfrey   Paper            $45.00
        Northwest   Pelfrey   Meat/Dairy      $205.00
        Northwest   Pelfrey   Canned          $420.00
        Northwest   Pelfrey   Produce          $76.00

                                            $2,454.00
```

Detail row

Default summary line for the whole report

**Ordered detail report with default and customized summaries.** If you order the rows of a detail report, you can include summaries for individual variables as well as for the whole report. This report orders rows within the Northeast sector alphabetically by the name of the manager. Within each manager's store, rows are ordered by department, according to internal values which place the departments selling nonperishable goods before the departments selling perishable goods. A default summary summarizes sales for each manager's store. A customized summary summarizes sales for all stores. A customized summary lets you control the content and appearance of the summary information, but you must write additional PROC REPORT statements to create one.

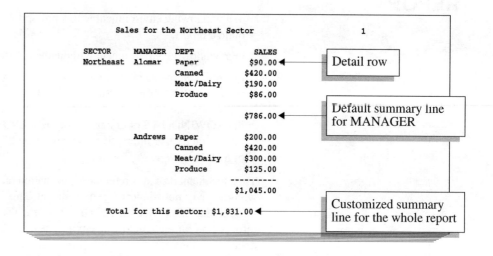

```
                    Sales for the Northeast Sector                        1

        SECTOR      MANAGER   DEPT              SALES
        Northeast   Alomar    Paper            $90.00
                              Canned          $420.00
                              Meat/Dairy      $190.00
                              Produce          $86.00

                                             $786.00

                    Andrews   Paper           $200.00
                              Canned          $420.00
                              Meat/Dairy      $300.00
                              Produce         $125.00
                                             ----------
                                           $1,045.00

            Total for this sector: $1,831.00
```

Detail row

Default summary line for MANAGER

Customized summary line for the whole report

**Summary report with a default summary.** This report contains one row for each manager's store. Each detail row represents four observations in the input data set — one for each department. Information about individual departments does not appear in this report. A default summary totals the sales for all the stores.

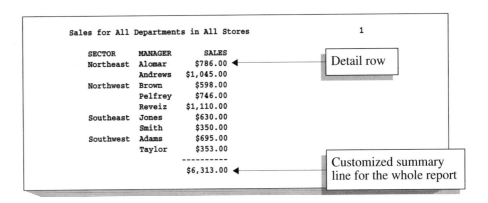

**Summary report with default and customized summaries.** This report contains one row for each store in the northern sector. Each detail row represents four observations in the input data set — one for each department. Information about individual departments does not appear in this report. A default summary totals the sales for each sector of the city. A customized summary totals the sales for both sectors.

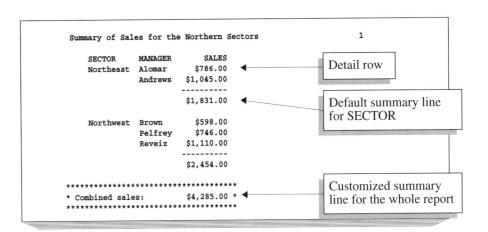

**Summary report.** This report is like the previous one except that it also includes information for individual departments.

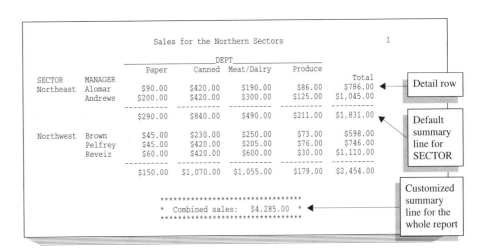

**Customized summary report.**
This customized report produces a report for each manager's store on a separate page. Only the first page appears here. This report includes a computed variable (PROFIT) that is not in the input data set.

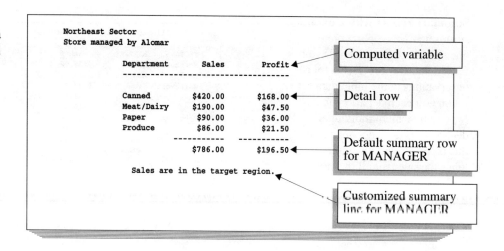

```
Northeast Sector
Store managed by Alomar

      Department        Sales        Profit
      ------------------------------------

      Canned           $420.00      $168.00
      Meat/Dairy       $190.00       $47.50
      Paper             $90.00       $36.00
      Produce           $86.00       $21.50
                      -----------  -----------
                        $786.00      $196.50

      Sales are in the target region.
```

Computed variable

Detail row

Default summary row for MANAGER

Customized summary line for MANAGER

**CHAPTER 2** **PROC REPORT Concepts**

*Report Layout* **5**
  *Usage of Variables in a Report* **6**
    *Display Variables* **6**
    *Order Variables* **6**
    *Across Variables* **7**
    *Group Variables* **7**
    *Analysis Variables* **7**
    *Computed Variables* **8**
  *Interactions of Position and Usage* **8**
  *Statistics Available in PROC REPORT* **10**
*Compute Blocks* **11**
  *The Purpose of Compute Blocks* **11**
  *The Contents of Compute Blocks* **12**
  *Four Ways to Reference Report Items in a Compute Block* **12**
  *Compute Block Processing* **13**
*Break Lines* **14**
  *Order of Break Lines* **14**
*Printing a Report* **15**
  *Printing from the REPORT Window* **15**
  *Printing with a Form* **15**
  *Printing from the OUTPUT Window* **15**
  *Printing from Noninteractive or Batch Mode* **15**
  *Printing from Interactive Line Mode* **16**
  *Using PROC PRINTTO* **16**
*Storing and Re-Using a Report Definition* **16**
*Using Form Characters* **16**
  *Default Form Characters* **17**
  *Changing Form Characters* **17**

## Report Layout

Report writing is simplified if you approach it with a clear understanding of what you want the report to look like. The most important thing to figure out is the layout of the report. To determine the layout, ask yourself the following kinds of questions:

☐ What do I want to display in each column of the report?

☐ In what order do I want the columns to appear?

☐ Do I want to display a column for each value of a particular variable?

☐ Do I want a row for every observation in the report, or do I want to consolidate information for multiple observations into one row?

☐ In what order do I want the rows to appear?

Once you have the layout of the report firmly in mind, use the COLUMN and DEFINE statements in PROC REPORT to construct the layout.

**The COLUMN statement** lists the items that appear in the columns of the report and describes the arrangement of the columns. A report item can be

☐ a data set variable

☐ a statistic calculated by the procedure

☐ a variable you compute based on other items in the report.

Omit the COLUMN statement if you want to include all variables in the input data set in the same order as they occur in the data set.

**Note:** If you start PROC REPORT in the windowing environment without the COLUMN statement, the initial report includes only as many variables as will fit on one page.

**The DEFINE statement** defines the characteristics of an item in the report. These characteristics include the column header, the format to use to display values, and how PROC REPORT uses the item in the report.

## Usage of Variables in a Report

Much of a report's layout is determined by the way that you use variables in the report. You tell PROC REPORT how to use a variable by specifying a usage in the DEFINE statement or DEFINITION window for that variable. For data set variables, these usages are

DISPLAY
ORDER
ACROSS
GROUP
ANALYSIS

A report can contain variables that are not in the input data set. These variables must have a usage of COMPUTED.

**Note:** All the examples referred to are in Chapter 3, "Syntax and Examples."

### Display Variables

A report that contains one or more display variables has a row for every observation in the input data set. Display variables do not affect the order of the rows in the report. If no order variables appear to the left of a display variable, the order of the rows reflects the order of the observations in the data set. By default, PROC REPORT treats all character variables as display variables.

Examples: 1, 2, 7

### Order Variables

A report that contains one or more order variables has a row for every observation in the input data set. If no display variable appears to the left of an order variable, PROC REPORT orders the detail rows according to the ascending, formatted values of the order variable. You can change the default order with ORDER= and DESCENDING in the DEFINE statement or the DEFINITION window.

If the report contains multiple order variables, PROC REPORT establishes the order of the detail rows by sorting these variables from left to right in the report. PROC REPORT does not repeat the value of an order variable from one row to the next if the value does not change.

Examples: 3, 8

## Across Variables

PROC REPORT creates a column for each value of an across variable. PROC REPORT orders the columns by the ascending, formatted values of the across variable. You can change the default order with ORDER= and DESCENDING in the DEFINE statement or the DEFINITION window.

    Columns created by across variables contain statistics or computed values. If no other variable helps define the column (see "COLUMN Statement" on page 33), PROC REPORT displays the N statistic (the number of observations in the input data set that belong to that cell of the report).

    **Note:** SAS users who are familiar with procedures that use class variables will see that across variables are class variables used in the column dimension.

Example:    5

## Group Variables

If a report contains one or more group variables, PROC REPORT tries to consolidate into one row all observations from the data set that have a unique combination of formatted values for all group variables.

    When PROC REPORT creates groups, it orders the detail rows by the ascending, formatted values of the group variable. You can change the default order with ORDER= and DESCENDING in the DEFINE statement or the DEFINITION window.

    If the report contains multiple group variables, the REPORT procedure establishes the order of the detail rows by sorting these variables from left to right in the report. PROC REPORT does not repeat the values of a group variable from one row to the next if the value does not change.

    **Note:** SAS users who are familiar with procedures that use class variables will see that group variables are class variables used in the row dimension.

Examples:    4, 5, 6, 9, 10, 11, 12, 13

▶ *Caution:  You cannot always create groups.*

PROC REPORT cannot consolidate observations into groups if the report contains any order variables or any display variables that do not have one or more statistics associated with them (see "COLUMN Statement" on page 33). In the windowing environment, if PROC REPORT cannot immediately create groups, it changes all display and order variables to group variables so that it can. In the nonwindowing environment, it returns a message and creates a detail report that displays group variables the same way as it displays order variables. Even if PROC REPORT creates a detail report, the variables that you defined as group variables retain that usage in their definitions.

## Analysis Variables

An analysis variable is a numeric variable used to calculate a statistic for all the observations represented by a cell of the report. (Across variables in combination with group variables or order variables determine which observations a cell represents.) You associate a statistic with an analysis variable in the variable's definition or in the COLUMN statement. By default, PROC REPORT uses numeric variables as analysis variables used to calculate the SUM statistic.

**In a detail report** the value of an analysis variable in a detail row is the value of the statistic associated with the variable calculated for a single observation. Calculating a statistic for a single observation is not practical; however, using the variable as an analysis variable enables you to create summary lines for sets of observations or for all observations.

**In a summary report** the value displayed for an analysis variable is the value of the statistic you specify calculated for the set of observations represented by that cell of the report.

**In a summary line** for any report, the value of an analysis variable is the value of the statistic you specify calculated for all observations represented by that cell of the summary line.

Examples: 3, 4, 5, 9, 12, 13
See also: BREAK statement
RBREAK statement

▶ *Caution:* *Using Dates in a Report*

Be careful using SAS dates in reports that contain summary lines. SAS dates are numeric variables. Unless you explicitly define dates as some other kind of variable, PROC REPORT will summarize them.

## Computed Variables

Computed variables are variables that you define for the report. They are not in the input data set, and PROC REPORT does not add them to the input data set. However, computed variables are included in an output data set if you create one.

In the windowing environment, you add a computed variable to a report from the COMPUTED VAR window.

In the nonwindowing environment, you add a computed variable by

□ including the computed variable in the COLUMN statement

□ defining the variable's usage as COMPUTED in the DEFINE statement

□ computing the value of the variable in a compute block associated with the variable.

Example: 5

## Interactions of Position and Usage

The position and usage of each variable in the report determine the report's structure and content. PROC REPORT orders the detail rows of the report according to the values of order and group variables, considered from left to right in the report. Similarly, PROC REPORT orders columns for an across variable from top to bottom, according to the values of the variable.

Several items can collectively define the contents of a column in a report. For instance, in Output 2.1 on page 9, the values that appear in the third and fourth columns are collectively determined by SALES, an analysis variable, and DEPT, an across variable. You create this kind of report with the COLUMN statement or by placing report items above or below each other. We sometimes refer to these items as being stacked in the report because each item generates a header, and the headers are stacked one above the other.

*Output 2.1*
*Stacking DEPT and SALES*

```
              Sales Figures for Perishables in Northern Sectors

                                  _____Department_____
                                 Meat/Dairy    Produce   Perishable
              Sector   Manager                              Total
              ------------------------------------------------------

              Northeast  Alomar    $190.00      $86.00     $276.00

                         Andrews   $300.00     $125.00     $425.00

              Northwest  Brown     $250.00      $73.00     $323.00

                         Pelfrey   $205.00      $76.00     $281.00

                         Reveiz    $600.00      $30.00     $630.00
```

When you use multiple items to define the contents of a column, you can have at most one of the following in a column:

□ a display variable with or without a statistic above or below it

□ an analysis variable with or without a statistic above or below it

□ an order variable

□ a group variable

□ a computed variable

□ the N statistic.

Having more than one of these items in a column creates a conflict for the REPORT procedure about which values to display.

Table 2.1 shows with which other items each type of report item can share a column.

**Note:** You cannot stack group or order variables with other report items.

*Table 2.1* *Report Items that Can Share Columns*

|  | **Display** | **Analysis** | **Order** | **Group** | **Computed** | **Across** | **Statistic** |
|---|---|---|---|---|---|---|---|
| Display |  |  |  |  |  | X* | X |
| Analysis |  |  |  |  |  | X | X |
| Order |  |  |  |  |  |  |  |
| Group |  |  |  |  |  |  |  |
| Computed variable |  |  |  |  |  | X |  |
| Across variable | X* | X |  |  | X | X | X |
| Statistic | X | X |  |  |  | X |  |

* When a display variable and an across variable share a column, the report must also contain another variable that is not in the same column.

The following items can stand alone in a column:

□ display variable

□ analysis variable

□ order variable

□ group variable

□ computed variable

□ across variable

□ N statistic.

**Note:** The values in a column occupied only by an across variable are frequency counts.

## Statistics Available in PROC REPORT

| N | RANGE | T |
|---|---|---|
| NMISS | SUM | PRT |
| MEAN | USS | VAR |
| STD | CSS | SUMWGT |
| MIN | STDERR | PCTN |
| MAX | CV | PCTSUM |

Every statistic except N must be associated with a variable. You do so either by placing the statistic above or below a numeric display variable or by specifying the statistic as a usage option in the DEFINE statement or DEFINITION window for an analysis variable.

You can place N anywhere because it is the number of observations in the input data set that contribute to the value in a cell of the report. The value of N does not depend on a particular variable.

Definitions of the statistics follow. The following notations are used where summation is over all nonmissing values:

$x_i$      the *i*th nonmissing observation on the variable.

$w_i$      the weight associated with $x_i$ if a WEIGHT statement is specified, and 1 otherwise.

$n$      the number of nonmissing observations.

$\bar{x}$      $\Sigma w_i x_i / \Sigma w_i$ .

$s^2$      $\Sigma w_i (x_i - \bar{x})^2 / (n - 1)$ .

$z_i$      $(x_i - \bar{x}) / s$ standardized variables.

The statistics are

**N**      the number of observations with no missing values for a group, order, or across variable; or the number of nonmissing values for an analysis variable.

         **Note:** If you use the MISSING option in the PROC REPORT statement, N includes observations with missing group, order, or across variables.

**NMISS**      the number of missing values for an analysis variable.

**MEAN**      $\bar{x}$, the arithmetic mean.

**STD**      *s*, the standard deviation.

| | |
|---|---|
| **MIN** | the minimum value. |
| **MAX** | the maximum value. |
| **RANGE** | MAX − MIN, the range. |
| **SUM** | $\Sigma\, w_i x_i$, the weighted sum. |
| **USS** | $\Sigma\, w_i x_i^2$, the uncorrected sum of squares. |
| **CSS** | $\Sigma w_i\,(x_i - \bar{x})^2$, the sum of squares corrected for the mean. |
| **STDERR** | $s\,/\sqrt{\Sigma w_i}$, the standard error of the mean. |
| **CV** | $100\, s\,/\bar{x}$, the percent coefficient of variation. |
| **T** | $t = \bar{x}\,\sqrt{n}\,/s$, Student's $t$ for $H_0$ : population mean=0. |
| **PRT** | the two-tailed $p$-value for Student's $t$ with $n - 1$ degrees of freedom, the probability under the null hypothesis of obtaining an absolute value of $t$ greater than the $t$-value observed in this sample. |
| **VAR** | $s^2$, the variance. |
| **SUMWGT** | $\Sigma w_i$, the sum of weights. |
| **PCTN** | the percentage of the total frequency count that the frequency count for a row represents. This percentage is expressed as a fraction. To view it as a percentage, use the PERCENT. format. |
| **PCTSUM** | the percentage of the sum for all rows in the report that the sum for a row represents. This percentage is expressed as a fraction. To view it as a percentage, use the PERCENT. format. |

# Compute Blocks

A compute block contains one or more programming statements that PROC REPORT executes as it builds the report. A compute block can be associated with a report item (a data set variable, a statistic, or a computed variable) or with a location (at the top or bottom of the report; before or after a set of observations). You create a compute block with the COMPUTE window or the COMPUTE statement. One form of the compute statement associates the compute block with a report item. Another form associates the compute block with a location (see "Break Lines" on page 14).

   **Note:**   When you use the COMPUTE statement, you do not have to use a corresponding BREAK or RBREAK statement. Use these statements only when you want to implement one or more BREAK statement or RBREAK statement options.

## The Purpose of Compute Blocks

A compute block that is associated with a report item can

□ define a variable that appears in a column of the report but is not in the input data set

□ define display attributes for a report item (see "CALL DEFINE Statement" on page 32).

A compute block that is associated with a location can write a customized summary.

   In addition, all compute blocks can use SAS language features to perform calculations (see "The Contents of Compute Blocks" on page 12). A PROC REPORT step can contain multiple compute blocks.

## The Contents of Compute Blocks

In the windowing environment, a compute block is in a COMPUTE window. In the nonwindowing environment, a compute block begins with a COMPUTE statement and ends with an ENDCOMP statement. Within a compute block, you can use these SAS language features:

□ DM statement

□ %INCLUDE statement

□ these DATA step statements:

| | |
|---|---|
| assignment | LENGTH |
| CALL | LINK |
| DO (all forms) | RETURN |
| END | SELECT |
| GO TO | sum |
| IF-THEN/ELSE | |

□ comments

□ null statements

□ macro variables and macro invocations

□ all DATA step functions.

For information on SAS language features see *SAS Language: Reference*.

Compute blocks also support these PROC REPORT features:

□ Compute blocks for a customized summary support the LINE statement, which lets you place customized text and formatted values in the summary.

□ Compute blocks for a report item support the CALL DEFINE statement, which lets you set attributes like color and format each time a value for the item is placed in the report.

For information on these features see "LINE Statement" on page 44 and "CALL DEFINE Statement" on page 32.

## Four Ways to Reference Report Items in a Compute Block

A compute block can reference any report item that forms a column in the report (whether or not the column is visible). You reference report items in a compute block in one of four ways:

□ by name.

□ by a compound name that identifies both the variable and the name of the statistic you calculate with it. A compound name has this form:

*variable-name.statistic*

□ by an alias that you create in the COLUMN statement or the DEFINITION
window

□ by column number, in the form

_Cn_

where *n* is the number of the column (from left to right) in the report.

▶ *Caution:* *Referencing*
*Variables with Missing Values*

If a compute block references a variable with a missing value, PROC REPORT
displays a blank (for character variables) or a period (for numeric variables).

................................................................................

The following table shows how to use each type of reference in a compute block.

| If the variable you reference is this type... | then refer to it by... | For example... |
|---|---|---|
| group | name[*] | DEPT |
| order | name[*] | DEPT |
| computed | name[*] | DEPT |
| display | name[*] | DEPT |
| display sharing a column with a statistic[*] | a compound name | SALES.SUM |
| analysis[*] | a compound name | SALES.MEAN |
| any type sharing a column with an across variable[**] | column number | _C3_ |

[*]If the variable has an alias, you must reference it with the alias.
[**]Even if the variable has an alias, you must reference it by column number.

Examples: 4, 5, 9, 10

## Compute Block Processing

PROC REPORT processes compute blocks in two different ways.

□ If a compute block is associated with a location, PROC REPORT executes the
compute block only at that location. Because PROC REPORT calculates statistics
for groups before it actually constructs the rows of the report, statistics for sets of
detail rows are available before or after the rows are displayed, as are values for
any variables based on these statistics.

□ If a compute block is associated with a report item, PROC REPORT executes the
compute block on every row of the report when it comes to the column for that
item. The value of a computed variable in any row of a report is the last value
assigned to that variable during that execution of the DATA step statements in the
compute block. Because PROC REPORT assigns values to the columns in a row
of a report from left to right, a computed variable can depend only on values to its
left.

For details on compute block processing see "How PROC REPORT Builds a
Report" on page 103.

# Break Lines

*Break lines* are lines of text (including blanks) that appear at particular locations, called *breaks*, in a report. A report can contain multiple breaks. Generally, break lines are used to visually separate parts of a report, to summarize information, or both. They can occur

□ at the beginning or end of a report

□ between sets of observations (whenever the value of a group or order variable changes).

Break lines can contain

□ text

□ values calculated for either a set of rows or for the whole report.

There are two ways to create break lines. The first way is simpler. It produces a default summary. The second way is more flexible. It produces a customized summary and provides a way to slightly modify a default summary.

Default summaries and customized summaries can appear at the same location in a report.

**Default summaries**   are produced with the BREAK statement, the RBREAK statement, or the BREAK window. You can use default summaries to visually separate parts of the report, to summarize information for numeric variables, or both. Options provide some control over the appearance of the break lines, but if you choose to summarize numeric variables, you have no control over the content and the placement of the summary information. (A break line that summarizes information is a summary line.)

**Customized summaries**   are produced in a compute block. You can control both the appearance and content of a customized summary, but you must write the code to do so.

## Order of Break Lines

You control the order of the lines in a customized summary. However, PROC REPORT controls the order of lines in a default summary and the placement of a customized summary relative to a default summary. When a default summary contains multiple break lines, the order in which the break lines appear is

□ overlining or double overlining

□ summary line

□ underlining or double underlining

□ blank line

□ page break

If you define a customized summary for the same location, customized break lines appear after underlining or double underlining.

# Printing a Report

## Printing from the REPORT Window

By default, if you print from the REPORT window, the report is routed directly to your printer. If you want, you can specify a form to use for printing (see "Printing with a Form"). Forms specify things like the type of printer that you are using, text format, and page orientation.

► *Caution:*   Forms are available only when you run SAS from display manager.

...................................................................

■ **Operating System Specifics**   Printing is implemented differently on different operating systems. For information related to printing, consult *SAS Language: Reference.* Additional information may be available in the SAS documentation for your operating system.

.......................................................................■

## Printing with a Form

To print with a form from the REPORT window:

□ Specify a form. You can specify a form with the FORMNAME command or, in some cases, through the "File" menu.

□ Specify a print file if you do not want to use the default. You can specify a print file with the PRTFILE command or, in some cases, through the "File" menu.

□ Issue the PRINT or PRINT PAGE command from the command line or from the "File" menu.

□ Free the print file. You can free a file with the FREE command or, in some cases, through "Print utilities" in the "File" menu. You cannot view or print the file until you free it.

□ Use operating system commands to send the file to the printer.

## Printing from the OUTPUT Window

If you are running PROC REPORT from display manager with the NOWINDOWS option, the default destination for the output is the OUTPUT window. Use the commands in the "File" pull-down menu to print the report.

## Printing from Noninteractive or Batch Mode

If you use noninteractive or batch mode, SAS writes the output either to the display or to external files, depending on the host system and the SAS options that you use. Refer to the SAS documentation for your host system for information on how these files are named and where they are stored.

You can print the output file directly or use PROC PRINTTO to redirect the output to another file. In either case, no form is used, but carriage control characters are written if the destination is a print file.

Use operating system commands to send the file to the printer.

## Printing from Interactive Line Mode

If you use interactive line mode, by default the output and log are displayed on the screen immediately following the programming statements. Use PROC PRINTTO to redirect the output to an external file. Then use operating system commands to send the file to the printer.

## Using PROC PRINTTO

PROC PRINTTO defines destinations for the SAS output and the SAS log (see Chapter 28, "The PRINTTO Procedure" *SAS Procedures Guide*).

PROC PRINTTO does not use a form, but it does write carriage control characters if you are writing to a print file.

▶ *Caution:* *You need two PROC PRINTTO steps.*

The first PROC PRINTTO step precedes the PROC REPORT step. It redirects the output to a file. The second PROC PRINTTO step follows the PROC REPORT step. It reestablishes the default destination and frees the output file. You cannot print the file until PROC PRINTTO frees it.

. . . . . . . . . . . . . . . . . . . . . . . . . . . . . . . . . . . . . . . . . . . . . .

# Storing and Re-Using a Report Definition

The OUTREPT= option in the PROC REPORT statement stores a report definition in the specified catalog entry. If you are working in the nonwindowing environment, the definition is based on the PROC REPORT step that you submit. If you are in the windowing environment, the definition is based on the report that is in the REPORT window when you end the procedure. The SAS System assigns an entry type of REPT to the entry.

In the windowing environment, you can save the definition of the current report by selecting

    File --> Save --> Report Definition

A report definition may differ from the SAS program that creates the report (see OUTREPT= in "PROC REPORT Statement" on page 20).

You can use a report definition to create an identically structured report for any SAS data set that contains variables with the same names as the ones used in the report definition. Use the REPORT= option in the PROC REPORT statement to load a report definition when you start PROC REPORT. In the windowing environment, load a report definition from the LOAD REPORT window by selecting

    File --> Open --> Report definition

# Using Form Characters

PROC REPORT uses the SAS system form characters to draw lines in its output. The BOX option (in the PROC REPORT statement and the ROPTIONS window) uses the characters to produce table outlines like those that PROC TABULATE produces. The underlining and overlining options that you can use when you create a default summary also use form characters.

When you start a SAS session, the system establishes default form characters. You can change these characters.

## Default Form Characters

The default form character string specifies the characters to use in linedrawing. You need to know the position of these characters in the formchar string if you want to change any of the characters. The following table supplies this information.

| Character name | Position in Formchar String | Default Character |
|---|---|---|
| Vertical bar | 1 | \| |
| Horizontal bar | 2 | - |
| Upper left intersection | 3 | - |
| Upper middle intersection | 4 | - |
| Upper right intersection | 5 | - |
| Middle left intersection | 6 | \| |
| Middle middle intersection | 7 | + |
| Middle right intersection | 8 | \| |
| Lower left intersection | 9 | - |
| Lower middle intersection | 10 | - |
| Lower right intersection | 11 | - |

## Changing Form Characters

The SAS system option FORMCHAR= specifies the default line-drawing characters. To change the characters that PROC REPORT uses, you must submit an OPTIONS statement before you start PROC REPORT. The general form of the FORMCHAR= option is

FORMCHAR='*formatting-characters*'

where *formatting-characters* is a list of characters. You can enter either a list of actual characters or a list of hexadecimal codes for the characters that you want to use.

Tip:      Consult the documentation for your printer to find the hexadecimal values for the characters that it can print.

Example:      8

▶ *Caution:*      If you replace characters that you cannot type from your keyboard, you will need to specify hexadecimal values for those characters if you reset the form character string.

. . . . . . . . . . . . . . . . . . . . . . . . . . . . . . . . . . . . . . . . . . . . . . . .

CHAPTER *3* # Syntax and Examples

*REPORT Procedure Syntax* **19**
*PROC REPORT Statement* **20**
*BREAK Statement* **28**
  *Order of Break Lines* **31**
*BY Statement* **32**
*CALL DEFINE Statement* **32**
*COLUMN Statement* **33**
*COMPUTE Statement* **35**
*DEFINE Statement* **37**
*ENDCOMP Statement* **43**
*FREQ Statement* **43**
*LINE Statement* **44**
    *Required Arguments* **44**
    *Differences between the LINE and PUT Statements* **45**
*RBREAK Statement* **45**
  *Order of Break Lines* **47**
*WEIGHT Statement* **48**
    *Required Arguments* **48**
*Examples* **48**
*Example 1* **49**
*Example 2* **51**
*Example 3* **52**
*Example 4* **55**
*Example 5* **57**
*Example 6* **60**
*Example 7* **61**
*Example 8* **63**
*Example 9* **65**
*Example 10* **68**
*Example 11* **70**
*Example 12* **72**
*Example 13* **74**

# REPORT Procedure Syntax

**PROC REPORT** <DATA=*SAS-data-set*> <OUT=*SAS-data-set*>
  WINDOWS I NOWINDOWS VARDEF=*divisor*
  <*layout-option(s)*>
  <*column-header-option(s)*>
  <*storage-and-retrieval-option(s)*>
  <*window-option(s)*>;
**BREAK** *location break-variable < / break-option(s) >*;
**COLUMN** *column-specification(s)* ;
**COMPUTE** *location < break-variable >*;
  **LINE** *specification(s)*;
  **ENDCOMP**;

# REPORT
## Procedure Syntax

*continued*

> **COMPUTE** *report-item* < / *type-specification* >;
>> **CALL DEFINE** (*column-id*, '*attribute-name*', *value*);
>> **ENDCOMP**;
>
> **DEFINE** *report-item* /<*usage* >
>> < *attribute(s)* >
>> < *option(s)* >
>> < *justification* >
>> < COLOR=*color* >
>> <'*column-header-1*' < ... '*column-header-n*'>>;
>
> **RBREAK** *location* < / *break-option(s)* >;
>
> **BY** <DESCENDING> *variable-1* < ... <DESCENDING> *variable-n* <NOTSORTED>;
> **FREQ** *variable*;
> **WEIGHT** *variable*;

# PROC REPORT
## Statement

> **PROC REPORT** <DATA=*SAS-data-set*> <OUT=*SAS-data-set*>
>> WINDOWS | NOWINDOWS
>> <*layout-option(s)*>
>> <*column-header-option(s)*>
>> <*storage-and-retrieval-option(s)*>
>> <*window-option(s)*>;

□ *layout-option(s)* can be one or more of the following:

| | |
|---|---|
| BOX | PS=*page-size* |
| CENTER \| NOCENTER | PSPACE=*space-between-panels* |
| COLWIDTH=*column-width* | SHOWALL |
| LS=*line-size* | SPACING=*space-between-columns* |
| MISSING | WRAP |
| PANELS=*number-of-panels* | |

□ *column-header-option(s)* can be one or more of the following:

| | |
|---|---|
| HEADLINE | NAMED |
| HEADSKIP | SPLIT='*character*' |
| NOHEADER | |

□ *storage-and-retrieval-option(s)* can be one or more of the following:

| | |
|---|---|
| LIST | PROFILE= |
| NOEXEC | REPORT= |
| OUTREPT= | |

□ *window-option(s)* can be one or more of the following:

| | |
|---|---|
| COMMAND | PROMPT |
| HELP=libref.catalog | |

## Options

BOX

uses the SAS system form characters to add line-drawing characters to the report. These characters

□ surround each page of the report

□ separate column headers from the body of the report

□ separate rows and columns from each other.

| | |
|---|---|
| Interaction: | You cannot use BOX if you use WRAP in the PROC REPORT statement or ROPTIONS window or FLOW in any item's definition. |
| More: | "Using Form Characters" |
| Example: | 12 |

CENTER | NOCENTER

specifies whether to center or left-justify the report and summary text (customized break lines).

PROC REPORT honors the first of these centering specifications that it finds:

1. the CENTER or NOCENTER option in the PROC REPORT statement or the CENTER toggle in the ROPTIONS window
2. the CENTER or NOCENTER option stored in the report definition loaded with REPORT= in the PROC REPORT statement
3. the SAS system option CENTER or NOCENTER.

| | |
|---|---|
| Interaction: | When CENTER is in effect, PROC REPORT ignores spacing that precedes the leftmost variable in the report. |

COLWIDTH=*column-width*

specifies the default number of characters for columns containing computed variables or numeric data set variables.

| | |
|---|---|
| Range: | 1 to the linesize |
| Default: | 9 |
| Interaction: | When setting the width for a column, PROC REPORT first looks at WIDTH= in the definition for that column. If WIDTH= is not present, PROC REPORT uses a column width large enough to accommodate the format for the item. (For information on formats see FORMAT= in "DEFINE Statement".) |

If no format is associated with the item, the column width depends on variable type:

| If the variable is a ... | then the column width is the ... |
| --- | --- |
| character variable in the input data set | length of the variable |
| numeric variable in the input data set | value of COLWIDTH= option |
| computed variable (numeric or character) | value of COLWIDTH= option |

Example:     2

**COMMAND**

displays command lines rather than menu bars in all REPORT windows. The option has no affect in the nonwindowing environment.

After you have started PROC REPORT, you can display the menu bars in the current window by issuing the COMMAND command. You can display the menu bars in all PROC REPORT windows by issuing the PMENU command. The PMENU command affects all the windows in your SAS session. Both these commands are toggles.

You can store a setting of COMMAND in your report profile. PROC REPORT honors the first of these settings that it finds:

□ the COMMAND option in the PROC REPORT statement

□ the setting in your report profile.

**DATA=***SAS-data-set*

identifies the input data set.

Examples:     All

**HEADLINE**

underlines all column headers and the spaces between them at the top of each page of the report.

The HEADLINE option underlines with the second character in the string defined by the SAS system option FORMCHAR=. Use the SAS system option FORMCHAR= to change it to another character.

Default:       –
Tip:           To underline column headers without underlining the spaces between them, use '--' as the last line of each column header instead of using HEADLINE.
Examples:     2, 4

**HEADSKIP**

writes a blank line beneath all column headers (or beneath the underlining that the HEADLINE option writes) at the top of each page of the report.

Example:     2, 4

**HELP=***libref.catalog*

identifies the library and catalog containing user-defined help for the report. This help can be in CBT or HELP catalog entries. You can write a CBT or HELP entry for each item in the report with the BUILD procedure in SAS/AF software. You must store all such entries for a report in the same catalog.

Specify the entry name for help for a particular report item in the DEFINITION window for that report item or in a DEFINE statement.

LIST
> writes to the SAS log the PROC REPORT code that creates the current report. This listing may differ in these ways from the statements that you submit:
>
> □ It shows some defaults that you may not have specified.
>
> □ It omits some statements that are not specific to the REPORT procedure, whether you submit them with the PROC REPORT step or previously. These statements include
>
> | | |
> |---|---|
> | BY | TITLE |
> | FOOTNOTE | WEIGHT |
> | FREQ | WHERE |
>
> □ It omits these PROC REPORT statement options:
>
> | | |
> |---|---|
> | LIST | REPORT= |
> | OUTREPT= | WINDOWS I NOWINDOWS |
> | PROFILE= | |
>
> □ It omits SAS system options.
>
> □ It resolves automatic macro variables.
>
> LIST has no effect in the windowing environment. Selecting
>
> | Locals | → | List REPORT statements |
>
> serves a similar purpose. It writes the report definition for the report currently in the REPORT window to the SOURCE window.

LS=*line-size*
> specifies the length of a line of the report.
> PROC REPORT honors the first of these linesize specifications that it finds:
>
> 1. the LS= option in the PROC REPORT statement or Linesize= in the ROPTIONS window
> 2. the LS= setting stored in the report definition loaded with REPORT= in the PROC REPORT statement
> 3. the SAS system option LINESIZE=.
>
> | | |
> |---|---|
> | Range: | 64-256 (integer) |
> | Example: | 6 |

MISSING
> considers missing values as valid values for group, order, or across variables. Special missing values used to represent numeric values (the letters A through Z and the underscore (_) character) are each considered as a different value. A group for each missing value appears in the report. If you omit the MISSING option, PROC REPORT does not include observations with a missing value for any group, order, or across variables in the report.
>
> | | |
> |---|---|
> | More: | For information on special missing values, see "Missing Values with Special Meaning" in Chapter 2 of *SAS Language: Reference.* |
> | Example: | 11 |

NAMED

writes *name*= in front of each value in the report, where *name* is the column header for the value.

| | |
|---|---|
| Tip: | Use NAMED in conjunction with the WRAP option to produce a report that wraps all columns for a single row of the report onto consecutive lines rather than placing columns of a wide report on separate pages. |
| Interaction: | When you use the NAMED option, PROC REPORT automatically uses the NOHEADER option. |
| Example: | 7 |

NOEXEC

suppresses the building of the report. Use NOEXEC with OUTREPT= to store a report definition in a catalog entry. Use NOEXEC with LIST and REPORT= to display a listing of the specified report definition.

NOHEADER

suppresses column headers, including those that span multiple columns.

Once you suppress the display of column headers in the windowing environment, you cannot select any report items.

| | |
|---|---|
| Example: | 9 |

OUT=*SAS-data-set*

creates an output data set from the data in the report. This data set contains one observation for each detail row of the report and one observation for each unique summary line. If you use both customized and default summaries at the same place in the report, the output data set contains only one observation because the two summaries differ only in how they present the data. Information about customization (underlining, color, text, and so forth) is not data and is not saved in the output data set.

The output data set contains one variable for each column of the report. PROC REPORT tries to use the name of the report item as the name of the corresponding variable in the output data set. However, this is not possible if a data set variable is under or over an across variable or if a data set variable appears multiple times in the COLUMN statement without aliases. In these cases, the name of the variable is based on the column number (_C1_, _C2_, and so forth).

Output data set variables that are derived from input data set variables retain the formats of their counterparts in the input data set. PROC REPORT derives labels for these variables from the corresponding column headers in the report unless the only item defining the column is an across variable. In that case, the variables have no label. If multiple items are stacked in a column, the labels of the corresponding output data set variables come from the analysis variable in the column.

The output data set also contains a variable named _BREAK_. If an observation in the output data set derives from a detail row in the report, the value of _BREAK_ is missing. If it derives from a summary line, the value of _BREAK_ is the name of the break variable associated with the summary line, or _RBREAK_.

| | |
|---|---|
| Interactions: | You cannot use OUT= in a PROC REPORT step that uses a BY statement. |
| Examples: | 12, 13 |

OUTREPT=*libref.catalog.entry*
> stores in the specified catalog entry the REPORT definition defined by the PROC REPORT step that you submit. PROC REPORT assigns the entry a type of REPT.
>
> The stored report definition may differ in these ways from the statements that you submit:
>
> □ It omits some statements that are not specific to the REPORT procedure, whether you submit them with the PROC REPORT step or whether they are already in effect when you submit the step. These statements include

| | |
|---|---|
| BY | TITLE |
| FOOTNOTE | WEIGHT |
| FREQ | WHERE |

> □ It does not include these PROC REPORT statement options:

| | |
|---|---|
| LIST | REPORT= |
| OUTREPT= | WINDOWS I NOWINDOWS |
| PROFILE= | |

> □ It omits SAS system options.
>
> □ It resolves automatic macro variables.
>
> Example:     7

PANELS=*number-of-panels*
> specifies the number of panels on each page of the report. If the width of a report is less than half of the line size, you can display the data in multiple sets of columns so that rows that would otherwise appear on multiple pages appear on the same page. Each set of columns is a *panel*. A familiar example of this kind of report is a telephone book, which contains multiple panels of names and telephone numbers on a single page.
>
> When writing a multipanel report, PROC REPORT fills one panel before beginning the next.
>
> The number of panels that fits on a page depends on the
>
> □ width of the panel
>
> □ space between panels
>
> □ linesize.
>
> Default:     1
> Tip:     If *number-of-panels* is larger than the number of panels that can fit on the page, PROC REPORT creates as many panels as it can. Let PROC REPORT put your data in the maximum number of panels that can fit on the page by specifying a large number of panels (for example, 99).
> See also:     For information on the space between panels and the linesize, see the discussions of PSPACE= and LS= in this section.
> Example:     8

PROFILE=*libref.catalog*
> identifies your REPORT profile. A profile
>
> □ specifies the location of menus that define alternative action bars and pull-down menus for the REPORT and COMPUTE windows.
>
> □ sets defaults for WINDOWS, PROMPT, and COMMAND.

PROC REPORT uses the entry REPORT.PROFILE in the catalog you specify as your profile. If no such entry exists, or if you do not specify a profile, PROC REPORT uses the entry REPORT.PROFILE in SASUSER.PROFILE. If you have no profile, PROC REPORT uses default menus and the default settings of the options.

You create a profile from the PROFILE window while using PROC REPORT in a windowing environment. To create a profile,

1. Invoke PROC REPORT with the WINDOWS option.
2. Select │Locals│ → │Display REPORT profile│
3. Fill in the fields to suit your needs.
4. Select OK to exit the PROFILE window. When you exit the window, PROC REPORT stores the profile in SASUSER.PROFILE.REPORT.PROFILE. Use the CATALOG procedure or the CATALOG window if you want to copy the profile to another location.

   **Note:** If you open the PROFILE window and decide not to create a profile, select CANCEL to close the window.

PROMPT

opens the REPORT window and starts the PROMPT facility. This facility guides you through creating a new report or adding more data set variables or statistics to an existing report.

If you start PROC REPORT with prompting, the first window gives you a chance to limit the number of observations used during prompting. When you exit the prompter, PROC REPORT removes the limit.

You can store a setting of PROMPT in your report profile. PROC REPORT honors the first of these settings that it finds:

□ the PROMPT option in the PROC REPORT statement

□ the setting in your report profile.

If you do not specify PROMPT in the PROC REPORT statement, the procedure uses the setting in your report profile, if you have one. If you do not have a report profile, PROC REPORT does not use the prompt facility.

PS=*page-size*

specifies the number of lines in a page of the report.

PROC REPORT honors the first of these page size specifications that it finds:

1. the PS= option in the PROC REPORT statement
2. the PS=setting in the report definition specified with REPORT= in the PROC REPORT statement
3. the SAS system option PAGESIZE=.

Range:      15-32,767 (integer)
Example:    6

PSPACE=*space-between-panels*

specifies the number of blank characters between panels. PROC REPORT separates all panels in the report by the same number of blank characters. For each panel, the sum of its width and the number of blank characters separating it from the panel to its left cannot exceed the line size.

Default:    4
Example:    5

REPORT=*libref.catalog.entry*
> specifies the report definition to use. PROC REPORT stores all report definitions as entries of type REPT in a SAS catalog.

| | |
|---|---|
| Interaction: | If you use REPORT=, you cannot use the COLUMN statement. |
| See also: | OUTREPT= earlier in this section. |

SHOWALL
> overrides options in the DEFINE statement that suppress the display of a column.

| | |
|---|---|
| See also: | NOPRINT and NOZERO in "DEFINE Statement" on page 37 |

SPACING=*space-between-columns*
> specifies the number of blank characters between columns. For each column, the sum of its width and the blank characters between it and the column to its left cannot exceed the line size.

| | |
|---|---|
| Default: | 2 |
| Interaction: | PROC REPORT separates all columns in the report by the number of blank characters specified by SPACING= in the PROC REPORT statement unless you use SPACING= in the DEFINE statement to change the spacing to the left of a specific item. |
| Interaction: | When CENTER is in effect, PROC REPORT ignores spacing that precedes the leftmost variable in the report. |
| Example: | 2 |

SPLIT='*character*'
> specifies the split character. PROC REPORT breaks a column header when it reaches that character and continues the header on the next line. The split character itself is not part of the column header although each occurrence of the split character counts toward the 40-character maximum for a label.

| | |
|---|---|
| Default: | / |
| Interaction: | The FLOW option in the DEFINE statement honors the split character. |
| Examples: | 2, 5 |

VARDEF=*divisor*
> specifies the divisor to use in the calculation of variances, where *divisor* can be

| | |
|---|---|
| DF | uses the degrees of freedom (N − 1) |
| N | uses the number of observations (N) |
| WDF | uses the sum of the weights minus 1 |
| WEIGHT | uses the sum of the weights. |

| | | |
|---|---|---|
| | Alias: | WGT |

| | |
|---|---|
| Default: | DF |

▶ *Caution:   Using a Divisor with the WEIGHT Statement*

> If you use a WEIGHT statement and you calculate variances or standard deviations, you may want to specify VARDEF=WDF. This provides an approximate estimate of the variance of an observation with average weight. However, this does not provide appropriate estimates of the mean or variance of the mean in stratified sampling situations.

WINDOWS | NOWINDOWS
> selects a windowing or nonwindowing environment.
> When you use WINDOWS, SAS opens the REPORT window, which enables you to modify a report repeatedly and to see the modifications immediately.

When you use NOWINDOWS, PROC REPORT runs without the REPORT window and sends its output to the SAS procedure output.

You can store a setting of WINDOWS in your report profile, if you have one. If you do not specify WINDOWS or NOWINDOWS in the PROC REPORT statement, the procedure uses the setting in your report profile. If you do not have a report profile, PROC REPORT looks at the setting of the SAS system option DMS. If DMS is ON, PROC REPORT uses the windowing environment; if DMS is OFF, it uses the nonwindowing environment.

| | |
|---|---|
| Alias: | WD I NOWD |
| See also: | For a discussion of the report profile see PROFILE= earlier in this section. |

### WRAP

displays one value from each column of the report, on consecutive lines if necessary, before displaying another value from the first column. By default, PROC REPORT displays values for only as many columns as it can fit on one page. It fills a page with values for these columns before starting to display values for the remaining columns on the next page.

| | |
|---|---|
| Interaction: | When WRAP is in effect, PROC REPORT ignores PAGE in any item definitions. |
| Tip: | Typically, you use WRAP in conjunction with the NAMED option to avoid wrapping column headers. |
| Example: | 7 |

# BREAK Statement

Produces a default summary at a break (a change in the value of a group or order variable). The information in a summary applies to a set of observations with a unique combination of values for the break variable and all other group or order variables to the left of the break variable in the report.

Examples: 4, 5

**BREAK** *location break-variable* < / *break-option(s)* >;

□ *break-option(s)* can be one or more of the following:

| | |
|---|---|
| COLOR=*color* | SKIP |
| DOL | SUMMARIZE |
| DUL | SUPPRESS |
| OL | UL |
| PAGE | |

## Required Arguments

*location*

controls the placement of the break lines and is either

AFTER     places the break lines immediately after the last row of each set of rows that have the same value for the break variable.

BEFORE    places the break lines immediately before the first row of each set of rows that have the same value for the break variable.

*break-variable*

is a group or order variable. The REPORT procedure writes break lines each time the value of this variable changes.

## Options

COLOR=*color*
specifies the color of the break lines. Currently, color appears only in the windowing environment. You can use the following colors:

| | | |
|---|---|---|
| BLACK | GRAY | PINK |
| BLUE | GREEN | RED |
| BROWN | MAGENTA | WHITE |
| CYAN | ORANGE | YELLOW |

Default: The color of "Foreground" in the SASCOLOR window. (See "SAS Global Color and Attribute Settings" in Chapter 1 of *SAS Software: Changes and Enhancements, Release 6.10*).

Note: Not all operating systems and devices support all colors, and on some operating systems and devices, one color may map to another color. For example, if the DEFINITION window displays BROWN in yellow characters, selecting BROWN results in a yellow item.

DOL
(for double overlining) uses the thirteenth character in the string defined by the SAS system option FORMCHAR= to overline each value

□ that appears in the summary line

□ that would appear in the summary line if you specified the SUMMARIZE option.

Default: equals sign (=)
Interaction: If you specify both the OL and DOL options, PROC REPORT honors only OL.
See also: "Changing Form Characters"

DUL
(for double underlining) uses the thirteenth character in the string defined by the SAS system option FORMCHAR= to underline each value

□ that appears in the summary line

□ that would appear in the summary line if you specified the SUMMARIZE option.

Default: equals sign (=)
Interaction: If you specify both the UL and DUL options, PROC REPORT honors only UL.
See also: "Changing Form Characters"

OL
(for overlining) uses the second character in the string defined by the SAS system option FORMCHAR= to overline each value

□ that appears in the summary line

□ that would appear in the summary line if you specified the SUMMARIZE option.

Default: hyphen (−)
Interaction: If you specify both the OL and DOL options, PROC REPORT honors only OL.
See also: "Changing Form Characters"
Example: 4

PAGE
:   starts a new page after the last break line.

    Interaction:   If you use PAGE in the BREAK statement and you create a break at the end of the report, the summary for the whole report is on a separate page.

    Example:   9

SKIP
:   writes a blank line for the last break line.

    Examples:   4, 5, 8

SUMMARIZE
:   writes a summary line in each group of break lines. A summary line for a set of observations contains values for

- the break variable (which you can suppress with the SUPPRESS option)
- other group or order variables to the left of the break variable
- statistics
- analysis variables
- computed variables.

The following table shows how PROC REPORT calculates the value for each kind of report item in a summary line created by the BREAK statement:

| If the report item is ... | then its value is ... |
| --- | --- |
| the break variable | the current value of the variable (or a missing value if you use SUPPRESS) |
| a group or order variable to the left of the break variable | the current value of the variable |
| a group or order variable to the right of the break variable, or a display variables anywhere in the report | missing* |
| a statistic | the value of the statistic over all observations in the set |
| an analysis variable | the value of the statistic specified as the usage option in the item's definition. PROC REPORT calculates the value of the statistic over all observations in the set. The default usage is SUM. |
| a computed variable | the results of the calculations based on the code in the corresponding compute block (see "COMPUTE Statement" on page 35). |

* If you reference a variable with a missing value in a customized summary line, PROC REPORT displays a blank (for character variables) or a period (for numeric variables).

**Note:** PROC REPORT cannot create groups in a report that contains order or display variables.

Example: 4

SUPPRESS

suppresses printing of

□ the value of the break variable in the summary line

□ any underlining and overlining in the break lines in the column containing the break variable.

**Note:** If you use SUPPRESS, the value of the break variable is unavailable for use in customized break lines unless you assign it a value in the COMPUTE block associated with the break (see "COMPUTE Statement" on page 35). Example: 4

UL

(for underlining) uses the second character in the string defined by the SAS system option FORMCHAR= to underline each value

□ that appears in the summary line

□ that would appear in the summary line if you specified the SUMMARIZE option.

Default:     hyphen (−)
Interaction: If you specify both the UL and DUL options, PROC REPORT honors only UL.
See also:    "Changing Form Characters"

# Order of Break Lines

When a default summary contains more than one break line, the order in which the break lines appear is

1. overlining or double overlining (OL or DOL)
2. summary line (SUMMARIZE)
3. underlining or double underlining (UL or DUL)
4. skipped line (SKIP)
5. page break (PAGE).

**Note:** If you define a customized summary for the break, customized break lines appear after underlining or double underlining. For more information on customized break lines, see "COMPUTE Statement" on page 35 and "LINE Statement" on page 44.

# BY Statement

**Creates a separate report for each BY group.**

**BY** <DESCENDING> *variable-1*
    <. . . <DESCENDING> *variable-n* >
    <NOTSORTED>;

When you use a BY statement, PROC REPORT expects the input data set to be sorted in order of the BY variables or to have an appropriate index.

| | |
|---|---|
| Interaction: | You cannot use the BY statement in the windowing environment. |
| Interaction: | If you use the RBREAK statement in a report that uses BY processing, the summary information is for each BY group. In this case, you cannot summarize information for the whole report. |
| Note: | Using the BY statement does not make the FIRST. and LAST. variables available in compute blocks. |

# CALL DEFINE Statement

**Sets the value of an attribute for a particular column in the current row.**

Valid only in a compute block that is attached to a report item.

Example: 4

The CALL DEFINE statement is often used to write report definitions that other people will use in a windowing environment. Only one attribute (format) has an effect in the nonwindowing environment. (See "Required Arguments" later in this section for a table describing available attributes.)

**CALL DEFINE** (*column-id*, '*attribute-name*', *value*);

## Required Arguments

*column-id*
    *column-id* specifies a column name or a column number. A column ID can be one of the following:

    □ a character literal (in quotation marks)

    □ a character expression.

    □ a numeric literal

    □ a numeric expression

    □ a name of the form _Cn_, where *n* is the column number

    □ the automatic variable _COL_. This variable identifies the column containing the report item that the compute block is attached to.

*attribute-name*
    is the attribute to define. For attribute names, refer to Table 3.1 on page 33.

*value*
    sets the value for the attribute. For values for each attribute, refer to Table 3.1 on page 33.

*Table 3.1*  *Attribute Descriptions*

| Attribute | Description | Values |
|-----------|-------------|--------|
| blink | Controls blinking of current value. | 1 turns blinking on; 0 turns it off. |
| color | Controls the color of the current value. | 'blue', 'red', 'pink', 'green', 'cyan', 'yellow', 'white', 'orange', 'black', 'magenta', 'gray', 'brown' |
| command | Specifies that a series of commands follows. | a quoted string of SAS commands to submit to the command line |
| format | Specifies a format for the column | a SAS format or a user-defined format |
| highlight | Controls highlighting of the current value. | 1 turns highlighting on; 0 turns it off. |
| rvsvideo | Controls display of the current value. | 1 turns reverse video on; 0 turns it off. |

**Note:**  The attributes BLINK, HIGHLIGHT, and RVSVIDEO do not work on all devices.

# COLUMN Statement

**Describes the arrangement of all columns and of headers that span more than one column.**

You cannot use the COLUMN statement if you use REPORT= in the PROC REPORT statement.

Examples: 1, 3, 5, 6, 9, 10, 13

**COLUMN** *column-specification(s)* ;

□ *column-specification(s)* is one or more of the following:

   *report-item(s)*

   *report-item-1, report-item-2 <. . . , report-item-n>*

   *('header-1' < . . .'header-n'> report-item(s) )*

   *report-item=name*

where *report-item* is the name of a data set variable, a computed variable, or a statistic. Available statistics are

| | | |
|-------|--------|--------|
| N | RANGE | T |
| NMISS | SUM | PRT |
| MEAN | USS | VAR |
| STD | CSS | SUMWGT |
| MIN | STDERR | PCTN |
| MAX | CV | PCTSUM |

## Required Arguments

*report-item(s)*
> identifies items that each form a column in the report.
> Examples:    1, 9, 13

*report-item-1, report-item-2 <. . . , report-item-n>*
> identifies report items that collectively determine the contents of the column or columns. We sometimes refer to these items as being stacked in the report because each item generates a header, and the headers are stacked one above the other. The header for the leftmost item is on top. If one of the items is an analysis variable, a computed variable, or a statistic, its values fill the cells in that part of the report. Otherwise, PROC REPORT fills the cells with frequency counts.
>
> If you stack a statistic with an analysis variable, the statistic that you name in the column statement overrides the statistic in the definition of the analysis variable. For example, the following PROC REPORT step produces a report that contains the minimum value of SALES for each sector.

```
proc report data=sasuser.grocery;
    column sector sales,min;
    define sector/group;
    define sales/analysis sum;
run;
```

> Note:          A series of stacked report items can include only one analysis variable or statistic. If you include more than one, PROC REPORT cannot determine which values to put in the cells of the report. It returns an error.
>
> Note:          You can use parentheses to group report items whose headers should appear at the same level rather than stacked one above the other.
>
> Examples:    5, 6, 10

*('header-1' <. . .'header-n'> report-item(s)*
> creates one or more headers that span multiple columns.
>
> *header*          is a string of characters that spans one or more columns in the report. PROC REPORT prints each header on a separate line. You can use split characters in a header to split one header over multiple lines. See the discussion of SPLIT= in "PROC REPORT Statement".
>
>                     If the first and last characters of a header are one of the following characters, PROC REPORT uses that character to expand the header to fill the space over the column or columns:
>
>                     —    =    _    .    *    +
>
>                     If the first character of a header is < and the last character is >, or vice-versa, PROC REPORT expands the header to fill the space over the column by repeating the first character before the text of the header and the last character after it.
>
>                     Example:   10
>
> *report-item(s)*    specifies the columns to span.

*report-item=name*
> specifies an alias for a report item. You can use the same report item more than once in a COLUMN statement. However, you can use only one DEFINE statement for any given name. (The DEFINE statement designates characteristics

such as formats and customized column headers. If you do not use a DEFINE statement for an item, the REPORT procedure uses defaults.)

Example:    3

   Assigning an alias in the COLUMN statement does not by itself alter the report. It enables you to use separate DEFINE statements for each occurrence of a variable or statistic.

▶ *Caution:*

When you refer in a compute block to a report item that has an alias, you must usually use the alias. However, if the report item shares a column with an across variable, you must reference it by column number (see "Four Ways to Reference Report Items in a Compute Block" on page 12).

· · · · · · · · · · · · · · · · · · · · · · · · · · · · · · · · · · · · · · · · · · · ·

# COMPUTE Statement

**Starts a *compute block*. A compute block contains one or more programming statements that PROC REPORT executes as it builds the report.**

An ENDCOMP statement must mark the end of the group of statements in the compute block.

You must specify either a location or a report item in the COMPUTE statement.

Examples: 3, 4, 5, 9, 10

A compute block can be associated with a report item or with a location (at the top or bottom of a report; before or after a set of observations). You create a compute block with the COMPUTE window or the COMPUTE statement. One form of the COMPUTE statement associates the compute block with a report item. Another form associates the compute block with a location.

> **COMPUTE** *location* < *break-variable* >;
>     **LINE** *specification(s)*;
>     **ENDCOMP**;
> **COMPUTE** *report-item* < / *type-specification* >;
>     **CALL DEFINE** (*column-id*, '*attribute-name*', *value*);
>     **ENDCOMP**;

You can also include some SAS language features in compute blocks (see "The Contents of Compute Blocks" on page 12).

## Required Arguments

*location*
   determines where the compute block executes.

   AFTER    executes the compute block at a break in one of the following places:

   □ immediately after the last row of a set of rows that have the same value for *break-variable*, or if there is a default summary on *break-variable*, immediately after the creation of the preliminary summary line (see Chapter 5).

   □ at the end of the report if you do not specify a break variable.

   BEFORE    executes the compute block at a break in one of the following places:

   □ immediately before the first row of a set of rows that have the same value for *break-variable*, or if there is a default summary on *break-variable*, immediately after the creation of the preliminary summary line (see "How PROC REPORT Builds a Report" on page 103).

              □ immediately before the first detail row if you do not specify a break variable.

              Example:   3

*report-item*
> specifies a data set variable, a computed variable, or a statistic to associate the compute block with. If you are working in the nonwindowing environment, you must include the report item in the COLUMN statement. If the item is a computed variable, you must include a DEFINE statement for it.
>
> Examples:   4, 5

▶ ***Caution:*** *Position of Computed Variables*

Because PROC REPORT assigns values to the columns in a row of a report from left to right, a computed variable can depend only on values to its left.

· · · · · · · · · · · · · · · · · · · · · · · · · · · · · · · · · · · · · · · ·

## Optional Arguments

*type-specification*
> specifies the type and, optionally, the length of *report-item.* If the report item associated with a compute block is a computed variable, PROC REPORT assumes that it is a numeric variable unless you use a type specification to specify that it is a character variable. A type specification has the form

              CHARACTER ‹LENGTH=*length*›

> where

| CHARACTER | specifies that the computed variable is a character variable. If you do not specify a length, the variable's length is 8. |
|---|---|
| | Alias:   CHAR |
| | Example:10 |
| LENGTH=*length* | specifies the length of a computed character variable. |
| | Default:   8 |
| | Range:   1 to 200 |
| | Interaction: If you specify a length, you must use CHARACTER to indicate that the computed variable is a character variable. |
| | Example:   10 |

*break-variable*
> is a group or order variable. If you specify a location (BEFORE or AFTER) for the COMPUTE statement, you can also specify a *break-variable.* When you specify a break variable, PROC REPORT executes the statements in the compute block each time the value of the break variable changes.

# DEFINE Statement

**Describes how to use and display the specified item. If you do not use a DEFINE statement, PROC REPORT uses default characteristics.**

Examples: 2, 3, 4, 5, 6, 9, 10

**DEFINE** *report-item* /<*usage*>
    < *attribute(s)* >
    < *option(s)* >
    < *justification* >
    < COLOR=*color* >
    <'*column-header-1*' < . . .' *column-header-n*'>>;

□ *usage* is one of the following:

| | |
|---|---|
| ACROSS | DISPLAY |
| ANALYSIS | GROUP |
| COMPUTED | ORDER |

□ *attribute(s)* can be one or more of the following:

FORMAT=*format*
ORDER=DATA|FORMATTED|FREQ|INTERNAL
SPACING=*horizontal-positions*
*statistic*
WIDTH=*column-width*

□ *option(s)* can be one or more of the following:

DESCENDING
FLOW
ID
NOPRINT
NOZERO
PAGE

□ *justification* is one of the following:

CENTER
LEFT
RIGHT

## Required Arguments

*report-item*
    specifies the name or alias (established in the COLUMN statement) of the data set variable, computed variable, or statistic to define.

**Note:**   Do not specify a usage option in the definition of a statistic. The name of the statistic tells PROC REPORT how to use it.

## Options

ACROSS

defines *item* as an across variable.

Example:     5

ANALYSIS

defines *item*, which must be a data set variable, as an analysis variable.

By default, PROC REPORT calculates the SUM statistic for an analysis variable. Specify an alternate statistic with the *statistic* option in the DEFINE statement.

**Note:**     Naming a statistic in the DEFINE statement implies the ANALYSIS option, so you never need to specify ANALYSIS. However, specifying ANALYSIS may make your code easier for novice users to understand.

Examples:     3, 4

CENTER

centers the formatted values of the specified item within the column width and centers the column header over the values. This option has no effect on the SAS system option CENTER.

COLOR=*color*

specify the color of the column header and the values of the item that you are defining. Currently, color appears only in the windowing environment. You can use the following colors:

| | | |
|---|---|---|
| BLACK | GRAY | PINK |
| BLUE | GREEN | RED |
| BROWN | MAGENTA | WHITE |
| CYAN | ORANGE | YELLOW |

Default:     The color of "Foreground" in the SASCOLOR window. (See "SAS Global Color and Attribute Settings" in Chapter 1 of *SAS Software: Changes and Enhancements, Release 6.10*).

Note:     Not all operating systems and devices support all colors, and on some operating systems and devices, one color may map to another color. For example, if the DEFINITION window displays BROWN in yellow characters, selecting BROWN results in a yellow item.

*column-header*

defines the column header for *item*. Enclose each header in single or double quotation marks. When you specify multiple column headers, PROC REPORT uses a separate line for each one. The split character also splits a column header over multiple lines.

Examples:     2, 4, 5
See also:     SPLIT= in "PROC REPORT Statement"
Default:

| Item | Header |
|---|---|
| variable without a label | variable name |
| variable with a label | variable label |
| statistic | statistic name |

If the first and last characters of a header are one of the following characters, PROC REPORT uses that character to expand the header to fill the space over the column.

$$- \quad = \quad . \quad * \quad +$$

If the first character of a header is < and the last character is >, or vice-versa, PROC REPORT expands the header to fill the space over the column by repeating the first character before the text of the header and the last character after it.

Tip:    If you want to use names when labels exist, submit the following SAS statement before invoking PROC REPORT:

options nolabel;

Tip:    HEADLINE underlines all column headers and the spaces between them. To underline column headers without underlining the spaces between them, use the special characters '--' as the last line of each column header instead of using HEADLINE (see Example 4).

COMPUTED
defines the specified item as a computed variable. Computed variables are variables that you define for the report. They are not in the data set, and PROC REPORT does not add them to the input data set.

In the windowing environment, you add a computed variable to a report from the COMPUTED VAR window.

In the nonwindowing environment, you add a computed variable by

□ including the computed variable in the COLUMN statement

□ defining the variable's usage as COMPUTED in the DEFINE statement

□ computing the value of the variable in a compute block associated with the variable.

Examples:    5, 10

DESCENDING
reverses the order in which PROC REPORT displays rows or values of a group, order, or across variable.

**Note:**    By default, PROC REPORT orders group, order, and across variables by their formatted values. Use the ORDER= option in the DEFINE statement to specify an alternate sort order.

DISPLAY
defines *item*, which must be a data set variable, as a display variable.

FLOW
wraps the value of a character variable in its column. The FLOW option honors the split character. If the text contains no split character, PROC REPORT tries to split text at a blank.

Example:    10

FORMAT=*format*

assigns a SAS or user-defined format to the item. This format applies to *item* as PROC REPORT displays it; the format does not alter the format associated with a variable in the data set. For data set variables, PROC REPORT honors the first of these formats that it finds:

1. the format assigned with FORMAT= in the DEFINE statement
2. the format assigned in a FORMAT statement when you start PROC REPORT
3. the format associated with the variable in the data set.

If none of these is present, PROC REPORT uses BEST*w*. for numeric variables and $*w*. for character variables. The value of *w* is the default column width. For character variables in the input data set, the default column width is the variable's length. For numeric variables in the input data set and for computed variables (both numeric and character), the default column width is the value specified by COLWIDTH= in the PROC REPORT statement or the ROPTIONS window.

In the windowing environment, if you are unsure what format to use, type a question mark (?) in the format field in the DEFINITION window to access the FORMATS window.

Example:     2

GROUP

defines *item* as a group variable.

Example:     4

ID

specifies that the item that you are defining is an ID variable. An ID variable and all columns to its left appear at the left of every page of a report. ID ensures that you can identify each row of the report when the report contains more columns than will fit on one page.

Example:     6

ITEMHELP=*entry-name*

references a HELP or CBT entry that contains help information for the selected item. Use PROC BUILD in SAS/AF Software to create a HELP or CBT entry for a report item. All HELP and CBT entries for a report must be in the same catalog, and you must specify that catalog with the HELP= option in the PROC REPORT statement or from the User Help fields in the ROPTIONS window.

Of course, you can access these entries only from a windowing environment. To access a help entry from the report, select the item and issue the HELP command. PROC REPORT first searches for and displays an entry named *entry-name*.CBT. If no such entry exists, it searches for *entry-name*.HELP. If neither a CBT nor a HELP entry for the selected item exists, the opening frame of the help for PROC REPORT is displayed.

LEFT

left-justifies the formatted values of *item* within the column width and left-justifies the column headers over the values. If the format width is the same as the width of the column, the LEFT option has no effect on the placement of values.

NOPRINT

suppresses the display of *item*. Use this option

□ if you do not want to show the item in the report but you need to use its values to calculate other values that you use in the report

□ to establish the order of rows in the report

□ if you do not want to use the item as a column but want to have access to its values in summaries (see Example 9).

Interaction: SHOWALL in the PROC REPORT statement or the ROPTIONS window overrides all occurrences of NOPRINT.

Examples: 3, 9, 12

NOZERO

suppresses the display of the item that you are defining if its values are all zero or missing.

Interaction: SHOWALL in the PROC REPORT statement or the ROPTIONS window overrides all occurrences of NOZERO.

ORDER

defines *item* as an order variable.

Example: 3

ORDER=DATA | FORMATTED | FREQ | INTERNAL

orders the values of a group, order, or across variable according to the specified order, where

DATA            orders values according to their order in the input data set.

FORMATTED       orders values by their formatted (external) values. By default, the order is ascending.

FREQ            orders values by ascending frequency count.

INTERNAL        orders values by the same sequence as PROC SORT would use. This sort sequence is particularly useful for displaying dates chronologically.

Default: FORMATTED

Interaction: DESCENDING in the item's definition reverses the sort sequence for an item.

Example: 3

▶ *Caution: Default for the ORDER= Option*

In other SAS procedures, the default is ORDER=INTERNAL. The default for the option in PROC REPORT may change in a future release to be consistent with other procedures. Therefore, in production jobs where it is important to order report items by their formatted values, specify ORDER=FORMATTED even though it is currently the default. Doing so ensures that PROC REPORT will continue to produce the reports you expect even if the default changes.

PAGE

inserts a page break just before printing the first column containing values of the selected item.

Interaction: PAGE is ignored if you use WRAP in the PROC REPORT statement or the ROPTIONS window.

RIGHT

> right-justifies the formatted values of the specified item within the column width and right-justifies the column headers over the values. If the format width is the same as the width of the column, RIGHT has no effect on the placement of values.

SPACING=*horizontal-positions*

> defines the number of blank characters to leave between the column being defined and the column immediately to its left. For each column, the sum of its width and the blank characters between it and the column to its left cannot exceed the line size.

| | |
|---|---|
| Default: | 2 |
| Interaction: | When PROC REPORT's CENTER option is in effect, PROC REPORT ignores spacing that precedes the leftmost variable in the report. |
| | SPACING= in an item definition overrides the value of SPACING= in the PROC REPORT statement or the ROPTIONS window. |

*statistic*

> associates a statistic with an analysis variable. You must associate a statistic with every analysis variable in its definition. PROC REPORT uses the statistic you specify to calculate values for the analysis variable for the observations represented by each cell of the report. You cannot use *statistic* in the definition of any other kind of variable.

> Default:     SUM

> **Note:**    PROC REPORT uses the name of the analysis variable as the default header for the column. You can customize the column header with the *column-header* option in the DEFINE statement.

> You can use the following values for *statistic* :

| | | |
|---|---|---|
| N | RANGE | T |
| NMISS | SUM | PRT |
| MEAN | USS | VAR |
| STD | CSS | SUMWGT |
| MIN | STDERR | PCTN |
| MAX | CV | PCTSUM |

| | |
|---|---|
| More: | For definitions of these statistics, see "Statistics Available in PROC REPORT" in Chapter 2. |
| Examples: | 3, 4 |

WIDTH=*column-width*
> defines the width of the column in which PROC REPORT displays *item*.

Range: 1 to the value of the LINESIZE= system option

Default: A column width that is just large enough to handle the format. If there is no format, PROC REPORT uses the value of COLWIDTH=.

Interaction: WIDTH= in an item definition overrides the value of COLWIDTH= in the PROC REPORT statement or the ROPTIONS window.

Example: 10

> **Note:** When you stack items in the same column in a report, the width of the item that is at the bottom of the stack determines the width of the column.

# ENDCOMP Statement

**Ends a compute block.**

A COMPUTE statement must precede the ENDCOMP statement.

**ENDCOMP**;

See also: COMPUTE statement

# FREQ Statement

**Treats observations as if they appear multiple times in the input data set.**

▶ *Caution: Frequency information is not saved.*

**FREQ** *frequency-variable*;

## Required Arguments

*frequency-variable*
> is a numeric variable in the input data set whose value represents the frequency of each observation. If you use the FREQ statement, PROC REPORT assumes that each observation in the input data set represents n observations, where n is the value of the FREQ variable. If n is not an integer, PROC REPORT truncates it. If n is less than 1 (which includes missing), PROC REPORT skips the observation.

> When you store a report definition, PROC REPORT does not store the FREQ statement.

# LINE Statement

**Provides a subset of the features of the PUT statement for writing customized summaries.**

Use only in a compute block associated with a location in the report.

You cannot use the LINE statement in conditional statements (IF-THEN, IF-THEN/ELSE, and SELECT) because it does not take effect until PROC REPORT has executed all other statements in the compute block.

Examples: 3, 9

**LINE** *specification(s)*;

## Required Arguments

*specification(s)*
> can have one of the following forms. You can mix different forms of specifications in one LINE statement.

> *item item-format*
>> specifies the item to display and the format to use to display it, where

>> | | |
>> |---|---|
>> | *item* | is the name of a data set variable, a computed variable, or a statistic in the report. For information on referencing report items see "Four Ways to Reference Report Items in a Compute Block" on page 12. |
>> | *item-format* | is a SAS or user-defined format. You must specify a format for each item. |

>> Examples:   3, 9

> *'character-string'*
>> specifies a string of text to display. When the string is a blank and nothing else is in *specification(s)*, PROC REPORT prints a blank line.

>> Example:   3

> *number-of-repetitions*'character-string'*
>> specifies a character string and the number of times to repeat it.

>> Example:   3

> *pointer-control*
>> specifies the column in which PROC REPORT displays the next specification. You can use either of the following forms for pointer controls:

>> | | |
>> |---|---|
>> | @*column-number* | specifies the number of the column in which to begin displaying the next item in the specification list. |
>> | +*column-increment* | specifies the number of columns to skip before beginning to display the next item in the specification list. |

>> Both *column-number* and *column-increment* can be either a variable or a literal value.

>> Examples:   3, 9

### Differences between the LINE and PUT Statements

The LINE statement does not support the following features of the PUT statement:

□ automatic labeling signaled by an equals sign (=), also known as named output

□ the _ALL_, _INFILE_, and _PAGE_ arguments and the OVERPRINT option

□ grouping items and formats to apply one format to a list of items

□ pointer control using expressions

□ line pointer controls (# and /)

□ trailing "at" signs (@ and @@)

□ format modifiers

□ array elements.

# RBREAK Statement

**Produces a default summary at the beginning or end of a report or at the beginning and end of each BY group.**

Example: 2

**RBREAK** *location* < / *break-option(s)* >;

□ *break-option(s)* can be one or more of the following:

| | | |
|---|---|---|
| COLOR=*color* | OL | SUMMARIZE |
| DOL | PAGE | UL |
| DUL | SKIP | |

### Required Arguments

*location*
  controls the placement of the break lines and is either

  AFTER     places the break lines at the end of the report.

  BEFORE    places the break lines at the beginning of the report.

### Options

COLOR=*color*
  specifies the color of the break lines. Currently, color appears only in the windowing environment. You can use the following colors:

| | | |
|---|---|---|
| BLACK | GRAY | PINK |
| BLUE | GREEN | RED |
| BROWN | MAGENTA | WHITE |
| CYAN | ORANGE | YELLOW |

  Default:   The color of "Foreground" in the SASCOLOR window. (See "SAS Global Color and Attribute Settings" in Chapter 1 of *SAS Software: Changes and Enhancements, Release 6.10*).

  Note:   Not all operating systems and devices support all colors, and on some operating systems and devices, one color may map to another color. For example, if the DEFINITION window displays BROWN in yellow characters, selecting BROWN results in a yellow item.

**DOL**

(for double overlining) uses the thirteenth character in the string defined by the SAS system option FORMCHAR= to overline each value

□ that appears in the summary line

□ that would appear in the summary line if you specified the SUMMARIZE option.

| | |
|---|---|
| Default: | equals sign (=) |
| Interaction: | If you specify both the OL and DOL options, PROC REPORT honors only OL. |
| More: | "Using Form Characters" |
| Example: | 2 |

**DUL**

(for double underlining) uses the thirteenth character in the string defined by the SAS system option FORMCHAR= to underline each value

□ that appears in the summary line

□ that would appear in the summary line if you specified the SUMMARIZE option.

| | |
|---|---|
| Default: | equals sign (=) |
| Interaction: | If you specify both the UL and DUL options, PROC REPORT honors only UL. |
| More: | "Using Form Characters" |

**OL**

(for overlining) uses the second character in the string defined by the SAS system option FORMCHAR= to overline each value

□ that appears in the summary line

□ that would appear in the summary line if you specified the SUMMARIZE option.

| | |
|---|---|
| Default: | hyphen (–) |
| Interaction: | If you specify both the OL and DOL options, PROC REPORT honors only OL. |
| More: | "Using Form Characters" |

**PAGE**

starts a new page after the last break line of a break located at the beginning of the report.

**SKIP**

writes a blank line after the last break line of a break located at the beginning of the report.

**SUMMARIZE**

includes a summary line as one of the break lines. A summary line at the beginning or end of a report contains values for

□ statistics

□ analysis variables

□ computed variables.

The following table shows how PROC REPORT calculates the value for each kind of report item in a summary line created by the RBREAK statement:

| If the report item is ... | then its value is ... |
| --- | --- |
| a statistic | the value of the statistic over all observations in the set |
| an analysis variable | the value of the statistic specified as the usage option in the DEFINE statement. PROC REPORT calculates the value of the statistic over all observations in the set. The default usage is SUM. |
| a computed variable | the results of the calculations based on the code in the corresponding compute block (see "COMPUTE Statement" on page 35). |

Example:    2

UL

(for underlining) uses the second character in the string defined by the SAS system option FORMCHAR= to underline each value

□ that appears in the summary line

□ that would appear in the summary line if you specified the SUMMARIZE option.

Default:        hyphen (−)

Interaction:   If you specify both the UL and DUL options, PROC REPORT honors only UL.

More:          "Using Form Characters"

## Order of Break Lines

When a default summary contains more than one break line, the order in which the break lines appear is

1. overlining or double overlining (OL or DOL)
2. summary line (SUMMARIZE)
3. underlining or double underlining (UL or DUL)
4. skipped line (SKIP)
5. page break (PAGE).

**Note:**   If you define a customized summary for the break, customized break lines appear after underlining or double underlining. For more information on customized break lines, see "COMPUTE Statement" on page 35 and "LINE Statement" on page 44.

### Information for the Windowing Environment

The RBREAK statement supports the COLOR= option in the windowing environment. For more information, see *SAS Guide to the REPORT Procedure*.

# WEIGHT Statement

**Weights the values of analysis variables when computing statistics.**

**WEIGHT** *weight-variable*;

## Required Arguments

*weight-variable*

The WEIGHT variable is a numeric variable in the input data set. PROC REPORT uses the value of the weight variable to calculate weighted statistics for each analysis variable. The WEIGHT variable need not be an integer and does not affect the degrees of freedom. If the value of weight variable is less than 0 (which includes missing), PROC REPORT uses a value of 0.

▶ *Caution:* *Weight information is not saved*

When you store a report definition, PROC REPORT does not store the WEIGHT statement.

# Examples

All but one of the examples use the data set SASUSER.GROCERY, which is created in the first example. All the examples use the permanent formats created in the first example.

Not every piece of code is explained in every example. For instance, in Example 2, a margin note explains the use of the RBREAK statement. Other examples that use a similar RBREAK statement do not have margin notes explaining it. To find an example that uses a feature that you are interested in, look up the feature's syntax. If there is an example illustrating that feature, its documentation points to the example.

These examples are all available through the online HELP for PROC REPORT. You can cut and paste the code from the help display into your SAS session, submit it as is, or modify it. In this way, you can experiment with PROC REPORT without having to do a lot of typing!

# Example 1

This report contains one row for every observation.

```
                    Sales for the Southeast Sector
                             for 08JUN95

                MANAGER  DEPT              SALES
                Smith    Paper            $50.00
                Smith    Meat/Dairy      $100.00
                Smith    Canned          $120.00
                Smith    Produce          $80.00
                Jones    Paper            $40.00
                Jones    Meat/Dairy      $300.00
                Jones    Canned          $220.00
                Jones    Produce          $70.00
```

*The data set SASUSER.GROCERY contains one day's sales figures for eight stores in the Grocery Mart chain. Each observation contains data for one department in one store. This data set is used for examples throughout this book.*

```
data sasuser.grocery;
   input sector $ manager $ dept $ sales @@;
   cards;
se 1 np1 50    se 1 p1 100    se 1 np2 120    se 1 p2 80
se 2 np1 40    se 2 p1 300    se 2 np2 220    se 2 p2 70
nw 3 np1 60    nw 3 p1 600    nw 3 np2 420    nw 3 p2 30
nw 4 np1 45    nw 4 p1 250    nw 4 np2 230    nw 4 p2 73
nw 9 np1 45    nw 9 p1 205    nw 9 np2 420    nw 9 p2 76
sw 5 np1 53    sw 5 p1 130    sw 5 np2 120    sw 5 p2 50
sw 6 np1 40    sw 6 p1 350    sw 6 np2 225    sw 6 p2 80
ne 7 np1 90    ne 7 p1 190    ne 7 np2 420    ne 7 p2 86
ne 8 np1 200   ne 8 p1 300    ne 8 np2 420    ne 8 p2 125
;
```

*PROC FORMAT creates permanent formats for SECTOR, MANAGER, and DEPT. The LIBRARY= option specifies a permanent storage location so that the formats are available in subsequent SAS sessions. These formats are used for examples throughout this book.*

```
proc format library=sasuser;
   value $sctrfmt 'se' = 'Southeast'
                  'ne' = 'Northeast'
                  'nw' - 'Northwest'
                  'sw' = 'Southwest';

   value $mgrfmt '1' = 'Smith'    '2' = 'Jones'
                 '3' = 'Reveiz'   '4' = 'Brown'
                 '5' = 'Taylor'   '6' = 'Adams'
                 '7' = 'Alomar'   '8' = 'Andrews'
                 '9' = 'Pelfrey';

   value $deptfmt 'np1' = 'Paper'
                  'np2' = 'Canned'
                  'p1'  = 'Meat/Dairy'
                  'p2'  = 'Produce';
run;
```

*The SAS system option FMTSEARCH= adds the SAS data library SASUSER to the search path that is used to locate formats.*

```
options nodate nonumber ps=18 ls=70 fmtsearch=(sasuser);
```

*The report contains a column for each item in the COLUMN statement.*

```
proc report data=sasuser.grocery nowd;
   column manager dept sales;
```

*The WHERE statement selects for the report only the observations for stores in the southeast sector.*

```
   where sector='se';
```

*The FORMAT statement assigns formats to use in the report. You can use the FORMAT statement only with data set variables.*

```
   format manager $mgrfmt.;
   format dept $deptfmt.;
   format sales dollar11.2;
```

*SYSDATE is an automatic macro variable that returns the date when the SAS job or SAS session began. The TITLE2 statement uses double rather than single quotes so that the macro variable resolves.*

```
   title 'Sales for the Southeast Sector';
   title2 "for &sysdate";
run;
```

# Example 2

This report contains one row for every observation and totals the values of SALES for the whole report. The text of the column headers is customized, and the split character controls the placement of line breaks in the column headers.

```
                    Sales for the Southeast Sector
                              for 08JUN95

          Store        Sector of
          Manager      the City      Department      Sales
          ------------------------------------------------------

          Smith        Southeast     Paper            $50.00
          Smith        Southeast     Meat/Dairy      $100.00
          Smith        Southeast     Canned          $120.00
          Smith        Southeast     Produce          $80.00
          Jones        Southeast     Paper            $40.00
          Jones        Southeast     Meat/Dairy      $300.00
          Jones        Southeast     Canned          $220.00
          Jones        Southeast     Produce          $70.00
                                                     =======
                                                     $980.00
```

*COLWIDTH=10 sets the default column width to 10 characters. SPACING= puts five blank characters between columns. HEADLINE underlines all column headers and the spaces between them at the top of each page of the report. HEADSKIP writes a blank line beneath the underlining that HEADLINE writes. SPLIT= sets the split character to '\*'.*

```
options nodate nonumber ps=18 ls=70 fmtsearch=(sasuser);
proc report data=sasuser.grocery nowd
            colwidth=10
            spacing=5
            headline headskip
            split='*';
    column manager sector dept sales;
```

*Text between single or double quotation marks in the DEFINE statement specifies the column header for that report item. The asterisk (\*) is the split character.*

```
define sector / 'Sector of*the City' format=$sctrfmt.;
define manager / 'Store*Manager' format=$mgrfmt.;
define dept / 'Department' format=$deptfmt.;
define sales / 'Sales' format=dollar7.2;
```

*This RBREAK statement produces a default summary at the end of the report. DOL writes a line of equal signs (=) above the summary information. SUMMARIZE sums the value of SALES for all observations in the report.*

```
rbreak after / dol summarize;
where sector='se';
title 'Sales for the Southeast Sector';
title2 "for &sysdate";
run;
```

# Example 3

This report orders rows alphabetically by manager. Within each set of rows for a manager, the departments are ordered so that sales for the two departments that sell nonperishable goods precede sales for the two departments that sell perishable goods.

The customized report summary displays the minimum and maximum values of SALES over all departments. To determine these values, PROC REPORT needs the MIN and MAX statistic for SALES in every row of the report. However, to keep the report simple, the display of these statistics is suppressed.

```
                    Sales for the Southeast Sector

            Manager  Department    Sales
            -------  ----------  -----------

            Jones    Paper          $40.00
                     Canned        $220.00
                     Meat/Dairy    $300.00
                     Produce        $70.00
            Smith    Paper          $50.00
                     Canned        $120.00
                     Meat/Dairy    $100.00
                     Produce        $80.00


      ------------------------------------------------------
     | Departmental sales ranged from $40.00 to $300.00.  |
      ------------------------------------------------------
```

*The column specifications SALES=SALESMIN and SALES=SALESMAX create aliases for the variable SALES. These aliases enable you to use SALES in three different columns of the report. Separate DEFINE statements for each alias create separate descriptions for each use of the variable.*

```
options nodate nonumber ps=18 ls=70 fmtsearch=(sasuser);
proc report data=sasuser.grocery nowd headline headskip;
   column manager dept sales
          sales=salesmin
          sales=salesmax;
```

*The values of all variables with the ORDER option in the DEFINE statement determine the order of the rows in the report. In this report, both MANAGER and DEPT are order variables. PROC REPORT orders the rows first by the value of MANAGER (because it is the first variable in the COLUMN statement) and then, within each value of MANAGER, by the values of DEPT.*

```
define manager / order
                 order=formatted
                 'Manager'
                 format=$mgrfmt.;
define dept    / order
                 order=internal
                 'Department'
                 format=$deptfmt.;
```

*The ORDER= option specifies the sort order for a variable. This report orders the values of MANAGER by their formatted values and orders the values of DEPT by their internal values (np1, np2, p1, and p2).*

*The value of an analysis variable in any row of a report is the value of the statistic associated with it (in this case SUM) calculated for all observations represented by that row. In a detail report each row represents only one observation. Therefore, the SUM statistic is the same as the value of SALES for that observation in the input data set. What you gain by using SALES as an analysis variable in this kind of report is the ability to summarize the values at the end of the report, where the SUM statistic is the sum for all rows of the report.*

```
define sales /analysis sum 'Sales' format=dollar7.2;
```

*These DEFINE statements use aliases from the COLUMN statement to calculate the MIN and MAX statistics for SALES. NOPRINT suppresses the printing of SALESMIN and SALESMAX. PROC REPORT has access to the variable's value so it can print them in the summary but it does not print those values in a column.*

```
define salesmin /analysis min noprint;
define salesmax /analysis max noprint;
```

This COMPUTE statement begins
a compute block that executes at
the end of the report. The first
LINE statement writes a blank
line. The second LINE statement
writes 53 hyphens (-), beginning
in column 11.

```
compute after;
   line ' ';
   line @11 53*'-';
```

The first line of this LINE
statement writes the text in
quotation marks, beginning in
column 11.

```
line @11 '| Departmental sales ranged from'
      salesmin dollar7.2  +1 'to' +1 salesmax dollar7.2
      '. |';
line @11 53*'-';
```

The second line writes the value
of SALESMIN with the
DOLLAR7.2 format. The
formatted value is displayed
beginning in the next column. The
cursor then moves one column to
the right (+1), where PROC
REPORT writes the text in
quotation marks. Again, the
cursor moves one column to the
right, and PROC REPORT writes
the value of SALESMAX with the
DOLLAR7.2 format.

The third line writes the text in
quotation marks, beginning in the
next column.

An ENDCOMP statement must
end a compute block.

```
endcomp;
   where sector='se';
   title 'Sales for the Southeast Sector';
run;
```

# Example 4

This example creates a summary report by consolidating information for each combination of sector and manager into one row of the report.

The report contains two default summaries: one summarizes sales for each sector; the other summarizes sales for all sectors.

Sales figures in detail rows use a format that does not include dollar signs. Sales figures in summary lines use dollar signs.

Column headers are customized, and the headers are underlined but the spaces between the columns are not.

```
         Sales Figures for Northern Sectors for 08JUN95

         Sector    Manager     Sales
         ---------  -------  ----------

         Northeast  Alomar       786.00
                    Andrews    1,045.00
                               ----------
                               $1,831.00

         Northwest  Brown        598.00
                    Pelfrey      746.00
                    Reveiz     1,110.00
                               ----------
                               $2,454.00

                               ==========
                               $4,285.00
```

```
options nodate pageno=1 ps=60 ls=72 fmtsearch=(sasuser);
  proc report data=sasuser.grocery nowd headskip;
     column sector manager sales;
```

*In this report, SECTOR and MANAGER are group variables. SALES is an analysis variable used to calculate the SUM statistic. Each detail row represents a set of observations that have a unique combination of formatted values for all group variables. The value of SALES in each detail row is the sum of SALES for all observations in the group.*

```
define sector / group format=$sctrfmt. 'Sector' '--';
define manager / group format=$mgrfmt. 'Manager' '--';
define sales / analysis sum format=comma10.2 'Sales' '--';
```

*The hyphen (-) is one of the special characters that PROC REPORT expands to fill the column if it is the first and last character of a header. Therefore, a header of two hyphens expands to fill the column and to underline the header above it without underlining the spaces between the columns.*

*The BREAK statement creates a default summary after the last row for each sector. OL writes a row of hyphens above the summary line. SUMMARIZE writes the value of SALES (the only analysis or computed variable) in the summary line. PROC REPORT sums the values of SALES for each group because SALES is an analysis variable used to calculate the SUM statistic. SUPPRESS suppresses the display of the break variable (SECTOR) from the summary line. SKIP writes a blank line after the summary line.*

```
break after sector / ol
                     summarize
                     skip
                     suppress;
rbreak after / dol summarize;
```

*In detail rows, PROC REPORT displays the value of SALES with the format specified in its definition (COMMA10.2). The compute block specifies an alternate format to use in the current column on summary rows. Summary rows are identified as having missing values for both MANAGER and SECTOR.*
***Note:** If SECTOR and MANAGER were both missing in a detail row, PROC REPORT would use the DOLLAR11.2 format in that row.*

```
compute sales;
   if manager=' ' and sector=' ' then
   call define(_col_,"format","dollar11.2");
endcomp;

title "Sales Figures for Northern Sectors for &sysdate";
where sector contains 'n';
run;
```

# Example 5

Like Example 4, this report consolidates multiple observations into one row. However, unlike Example 4, which does not distinguish sales by department, this report contains a column for each value of DEPT that is selected for the report (the departments that sell perishable items).

This report contains a variable that is not in the input data set. The variable is computed from the values of SALES in the two departments that are included in the report.

Some, but not all, of the headers in this report contain blank lines.

The report is double-spaced.

```
            Sales Figures for Perishables in Northern Sectors

                             _____Department_____
      Sector    Manager   Meat/Dairy     Produce    Perishable
                                                        Total
      ------------------------------------------------------------

      Northeast Alomar       $190.00      $86.00      $276.00

                Andrews      $300.00     $125.00      $425.00

      Northwest Brown        $250.00      $73.00      $323.00

                Pelfrey      $205.00      $76.00      $281.00

                Reveiz       $600.00      $30.00      $630.00
```

*SPLIT= defines the split character as an asterisk (\*). The default split character is the forward slash (/). This report must use an alternate split character because one of the column headers (Meat/Dairy) contains a forward slash. If the report used the default split character, that column header would split over two lines and PROC REPORT would not print the forward slash.*

```
options nodate pageno=1 ps=60 ls=72 fmtsearch=(sasuser);
proc report data=sasuser.grocery nowd headskip headline split='*';
```

*DEPT and SALES are separated by a comma in the COLUMN statement, so they collectively determine the contents of the column that they define. Each item generates a header, but the header for SALES is set to blank in its definition. Because SALES is an analysis variable, its values fill the cells created by these two variables.*

```
column sector manager dept,sales perish;
```

*There are two ways to write a blank line in a column header. **'Sector' ''** writes a blank line because each quoted string is a line of the column header. The two adjacent quotation marks write a blank line for the second line of the header. **'Manager\* '** writes a blank line because the split character (\*) starts a new line of the header. That line contains only a blank.*

```
define sector / group format=$sctrfmt. 'Sector' '';
define manager / group format=$mgrfmt. 'Manager* ';
```

*PROC REPORT creates a column and a column header for each formatted value of the across variable DEPT. Each column header is a formatted value of the variable. PROC REPORT orders the columns by these values. PROC REPORT also generates a column header that spans all these columns. Quoted text in the DEFINE statement for DEPT customizes this header. PROC REPORT expands the header with underscores to fill all columns created by the across variable.*

```
define dept / across format=$deptfmt. '_Department_';
define sales / analysis sum format=dollar11.2 ' ';
```

*The COMPUTED argument indicates that PROC REPORT must compute values for PERISH. You compute the variable's values in a compute block associated with PERISH.*

```
define perish / computed format=dollar11.2 'Perishable Total';
```

*This BREAK statement creates a default summary after the last row for each value of MANAGER. The only option in use is SKIP, which writes a blank line. You can use this technique to double-space in many reports that contains a group or order variable.*

```
break after manager / skip;
```

*This compute block computes the value of PERISH from the values for the Meat/Dairy department and the Produce department. Because the variables SALES and DEPT collectively define these columns, there is no way to identify the values to PROC REPORT by name. Therefore, the assignment statement uses column numbers to unambiguously specify the values to use. Each time PROC REPORT needs a value for PERISH, it sums the values in the third and fourth columns of that row of the report.*

```
compute perish;
   perish=_c3_+_c4_;
endcomp;
title "Sales Figures for Perishables in Northern Sectors";
where sector contains 'n' and (dept='p1' or dept='p2');
run;
```

# Example 6

This report displays six statistics for the sales for each manager's store. The output is too wide to fit all the columns on one page, so three of the statistics appear on the second page of the report. In order to make it easy to associate the statistics on the second page with their group, the report repeats the values of MANAGER and SECTOR on every page of the report.

```
                    Sales Statistics for All Sectors                    1

                              SUM          MIN          MAX
            SECTOR     MANAGER      SALES        SALES        SALES
            --------------------------------------------------------------

            Northeast  Alomar      $786.00       $86.00      $420.00
                       Andrews   $1,045.00      $125.00      $430.00
            Northwest  Brown       $598.00       $45.00      $250.00
                       Pelfrey     $746.00       $45.00      $420.00
                       Reveiz    $1,110.00       $30.00      $600.00
            Southeast  Jones       $630.00       $40.00      $300.00
                       Smith       $350.00       $50.00      $120.00
            Southwest  Adams       $695.00       $40.00      $350.00
                       Taylor      $353.00       $50.00      $130.00
```

```
                    Sales Statistics for All Sectors                    2

                             RANGE         MEAN          STD
            SECTOR     MANAGER      SALES        SALES        SALES
            --------------------------------------------------------------

            Northeast  Alomar      $334.00      $196.50      $156.57
                       Andrews     $295.00      $261.25      $127.83
            Northwest  Brown       $205.00      $149.50      $105.44
                       Pelfrey     $375.00      $186.50      $170.39
                       Reveiz      $570.00      $277.50      $278.61
            Southeast  Jones       $260.00      $157.50      $123.39
                       Smith        $70.00       $87.50       $29.86
            Southwest  Adams       $310.00      $173.75      $141.86
                       Taylor       $80.00       $88.25       $42.65
```

*LS= and PS= set the linesize and pagesize for the report. Their values override the settings of the SAS system options LINESIZE= and PAGESIZE= while PROC REPORT is running. After PROC REPORT terminates, the system options resume control of the linesize and the pagesize.*

```
options number pageno=1 fmtsearch=(sasuser);
proc report data=sasuser.grocery nowd headline headskip
            ls=66 ps=18;
```

*An analysis variable must have one or more statistics associated with it. In this report SALES is, by default, an analysis variable used to calculate the SUM statistic. However, the structure of the COLUMN statement associates six statistics with SALES. PROC REPORT creates a column for each statistic. When you associate statistics with an analysis variable in the COLUMN statement, a statistic in the analysis variable's definition does not appear in the report unless it is also in the COLUMN statement.*

```
column sector manager (sum min max range mean std),sales;
```

*ID specifies that MANAGER is an ID variable. An ID variable and all columns to its left appear at the left of every page of a report. ID ensures that you can identify each row of the report when the report contains more columns than will fit on one page.*

```
      define manager/group format=$mgrfmt. id;
      define sector/group format=$sctrfmt.;
      define sales / format=dollar11.2 ;
      title 'Sales Statistics for All Sectors';
   run;
```

# Example 7

The first PROC REPORT step in this example creates a report that displays one value from each column of the report, using two rows to do so, before displaying another value from the first column. (By default, PROC REPORT displays values for only as many columns as it can fit on one page. It fills a page with values for these columns before starting to display values for the remaining columns on the next page.)

Each item in the report is identified in the body of the report rather than in a column header.

The report definition created by the first PROC REPORT step is stored in a catalog entry. The second PROC REPORT step uses it to create a similar report for a different sector of the city.

*This is the output from the first PROC REPORT step, which creates the report definition.*

```
                  Sales Figures for Smith on 08JUN95

       SECTOR=Southeast  MANAGER=Smith      DEPT=Paper
       SALES=     $50.00
       SECTOR=Southeast  MANAGER=Smith      DEPT=Meat/Dairy
       SALES=    $100.00
       SECTOR=Southeast  MANAGER=Smith      DEPT=Canned
       SALES=    $120.00
       SECTOR=Southeast  MANAGER=Smith      DEPT=Produce
       SALES=     $80.00
```

*This is the output from the second PROC REPORT step, which uses the same report definition with a different WHERE statement.*

```
        Sales Figures for the Southwest Sector on 08JUN95

        SECTOR=Southwest   MANAGER=Taylor    DEPT=Paper
        SALES=      $53.00
        SECTOR=Southwest   MANAGER=Taylor    DEPT=Meat/Dairy
        SALES=     $130.00
        SECTOR=Southwest   MANAGER=Taylor    DEPT=Canned
        SALES=     $120.00
        SECTOR=Southwest   MANAGER=Taylor    DEPT=Produce
        SALES=      $50.00
        SECTOR=Southwest   MANAGER=Adams     DEPT=Paper
        SALES=      $40.00
        SECTOR=Southwest   MANAGER=Adams     DEPT=Meat/Dairy
        SALES=     $350.00
        SECTOR=Southwest   MANAGER=Adams     DEPT=Canned
        SALES=     $225.00
        SECTOR=Southwest   MANAGER=Adams     DEPT=Produce
        SALES=      $80.00
```

*NAMED writes **name=** in front of each value in the report, where **name** is the column header for the value. When you use NAMED, PROC REPORT suppresses the display of column headers at the top of each page.*

```
options nodate nonumber fmtsearch=(sasuser);
proc report data=sasuser.grocery nowd
            named
            wrap
            ls=64 ps=18
            outrept=sasuser.reports.namewrap;
    column sector manager dept sales;
    define sector / format=$sctrfmt.;
    define manager / format=$mgrfmt.;
    define dept / format=$deptfmt.;
    define sales / format=dollar11.2;
```

*WRAP displays one value from each column of the report before displaying another value from the first column. Without WRAP, PROC REPORT would place the values for SALES in a column on a separate page.*

*OUTREPT= stores a report definition in the catalog entry SASUSER.REPORTS.NAMEWRAP.REPT. (PROC REPORT assigns the entry type.) You can use the report definition to produce a similar report for any data set containing the variables in the COLUMN statement.*

*A report definition may differ from the SAS program that creates the report. In particular, PROC REPORT stores neither WHERE statements nor TITLE statements.*

```
    where manager='1';
    title "Sales Figures for Smith on &sysdate";
run;
```

*REPORT= uses the report definition stored in SASUSER.REPORTS.NAMEWRAP to produce the report. The second report differs from the first one because it uses different WHERE and TITLE statements.*

```
proc report data=sasuser.grocery report=sasuser.reports.namewrap
            nowd;
   where sector='sw';
   title "Sales Figures for the Southwest Sector on &sysdate";
run;
```

# Example 8

This report uses panels to condense a two-page report to one page. Panels compactly present information for long, narrow reports by placing multiple rows of information side by side.

The SAS system option FORMCHAR= changes the underlining character (the second form character) for the duration of this PROC REPORT step.

A default summary places a blank line after the last row for each manager.

```
                       Sales for the Western Sectors

        Manager  Department    Sales      Manager  Department    Sales
        ~~~~~~~~~~~~~~~~~~~~~~~~~~~~~~     ~~~~~~~~~~~~~~~~~~~~~~~~~~~~~~
        Adams    Paper        $40.00
                 Canned      $225.00      Reveiz   Paper        $60.00
                 Meat/Dairy  $350.00               Canned      $420.00
                 Produce      $80.00               Meat/Dairy  $600.00
                                                   Produce      $30.00
        Brown    Paper        $45.00
                 Canned      $230.00      Taylor   Paper        $53.00
                 Meat/Dairy  $250.00               Canned      $120.00
                 Produce      $73.00               Meat/Dairy  $130.00
                                                   Produce      $50.00
        Pelfrey  Paper        $45.00
                 Canned      $420.00
                 Meat/Dairy  $205.00
                 Produce      $76.00
```

*By default, HEADLINE underlines with the second character in the string defined by the SAS system option FORMCHAR=. This use of FORMCHAR= option sets the value of this character to the tilde (~). Therefore, the tilde underlines the column headers in the output.*

```
options nodate nonumber fmtsearch=(sasuser);
options formchar='|~---|+|---+=|-/<>*';
```

*PANELS— creates a multipanel report. Specifying PANELS=99 ensures that PROC REPORT fits as many panels as possible on one page.*

```
proc report data=sasuser.grocery nowd headline
            panels=99 pspace=8
            ps=18 ls=68;
  column manager dept sales;
  define manager/ order order-formatted format=$mgrfmt. 'Manager';
  define dept / order order=internal format=$deptfmt.
                'Department';
  define sales / format=dollar7.2 'Sales';
```

*SKIP writes a blank line after the last row for each manager.*

```
  break after manager / skip;
  where sector='nw' or sector='sw';
  title "Sales for the Western Sectors";
run;
```

*This use of FORMCHAR= resets the value of the second form character to the hyphen (-), which is the default in the SAS session used to create this example.*

```
options formchar='|----|+|---+=|-/<>*';
```

# Example 9

This report displays a record of one day's sales for each store. The rows are arranged so that all the information about one store is together, and the information for each store begins on a new page. Some variables appear in columns. Others appear only in the page header that identifies the sector and the store's manager.

The default column headers are replaced by customized column headers that appear between the page header and the data.

PROFIT is a computed variable based on the value of SALES and DEPT.

The text that appears at the bottom of the page depends on the total of SALES for the store. Only the first two pages of the report appear here.

```
Northeast Sector
Store managed by Alomar


            Department      Sales      Profit
            -----------------------------------

            Canned         $420.00     $168.00
            Meat/Dairy     $190.00      $47.50
            Paper           $90.00      $36.00
            Produce         $86.00      $21.50
                           ----------  ----------
                           $786.00     $196.50

            Sales are in the target region.
```

```
Northeast Sector
Store managed by Andrews


            Department      Sales      Profit
            -----------------------------------

            Canned         $420.00     $168.00
            Meat/Dairy     $300.00      $75.00
            Paper          $200.00      $80.00
            Produce        $125.00      $31.25
                           ----------  ----------
                           $1,045.00   $261.25

               SALES EXCEEDED GOAL!
```

By default, PROC REPORT writes column headers at the top of each page. These column headers come before any customized summaries. In this report, you want the page header (which is a customized summary) to appear before the column headers. Therefore, you must replace the default column headers with customized headers that appear after the page header. NOHEADER in the PROC REPORT statement suppresses the default column headers. Customized column headers are created later in the PROC REPORT step.

```
options nodate pageno=1 ps=60 ls=66 fmtsearch=(sasuser);
proc report data=sasuser.grocery nowd
             noheader;
   title;
```

Each page header identifies the store whose sales are on that page. The header contains text that is the same on all pages and variable values for SECTOR and MANAGER that differ on each page. SECTOR and MANAGER do not appear in columns in the report. In order to get variable values in the page header, you must include the variables in the COLUMN statement. To prevent them from appearing in columns, use NOPRINT in their definitions.

```
column sector manager dept sales profit;
define sector / group noprint;
define manager / group noprint;
define profit / computed format=dollar11.2;
define sales / analysis sum format=dollar11.2;
define dept / group format=$deptfmt.;
```

PROFIT is computed as a percentage of SALES. For nonperishable items, the profit is 40% of the sale price. For perishable items the profit is 25%. Notice the use of the compound name SALES.SUM in the statements that compute PROFIT. When you base a computed variable on an analysis variable, you must use a name that identifies both the variable and the statistic that you calculate with it.

```
compute profit;
   if dept='np1' or dept='np2' then profit=0.4*sales.sum;
   else profit=0.25*sales.sum;
endcomp;
```

*This compute block executes before the first row for each value of MANAGER. It writes the page header for that manager's store. Each LINE statement writes the text in quotation marks just as it appears in the statement. It writes a variable value with the format specified immediately after the variable's name. The @ specifies the column to write in. The + indicates how many columns to move the pointer before continuing to write.*

```
compute before manager;
    line @3 sector $sctrfmt. ' Sector';
    line @3 'Store managed by ' manager $mgrfmt.;
    line ' ';
    line ' ';
    line @16 'Department' +7 'Sales' +8 'Profit';
    line @16 36*'-';
    line ' ';
endcomp;
```

*Because the default summary after the last row for each manager includes PAGE, the page header created in the preceding compute block is always at the top of a new page.*

```
break after manager / ol summarize page;
```

*This compute block places conditional text in a customized summary that appears after the last detail row for each manager.*

```
compute after manager;
```

*A character variable takes its length from the first value assigned to it unless a LENGTH statement precedes the first use of the variable. In situations like this one, it is wise to assign a length that will accommodate the longest version of the conditional text. In this particular case, the LENGTH statement is unnecessary because the longest version appears in the first IF/THEN statement. However, using the LENGTH statement ensures that even if the order of the conditional statements changes, TEXT will be long enough to hold the longest version.*

```
    length text $ 35;
```

*You cannot use the LINE statement in conditional statements (IF-THEN, IF-THEN/ELSE, and SELECT) because it does not take effect until PROC REPORT has executed all other statements in the compute block. These IF-THEN/ELSE statements assign a value to TEXT based on the value of SALES.SUM in the summary row. A LINE statement writes that variable, whatever its value happens to be.*

```
if sales.sum lt 500 then
    text='Sales are below the target region.';
else if sales.sum ge 500 and sales.sum lt 1000 then
    text='Sales are in the target region.';
else if sales.sum ge 1000 then
    text='SALES EXCEEDED GOAL!';
line ' ';
line text $35.;
endcomp;
run;
```

# Example 10

This summary report shows the total sales for each store and the percentage that these sales represent of sales for all stores. Each of these columns has its own header. A single header also spans all the columns. This header looks like a title, but it differs from a title because it would be stored in a report definition. You must submit a null TITLE statement whenever you use the report definition, or the report will contain both a title and the spanning header.

The report includes a computed character variable, COMMENT, that flags stores with an unusually high percentage of sales. The text of COMMENT wraps across multiple rows. It makes sense to compute COMMENT only for individual stores. Therefore, the compute block that does the calculation includes conditional code that prevents PROC REPORT from calculating COMMENT on the summary line.

```
              Individual Store Sales as a Percent of All Sales

                            Total    Percent
          Sector   Manager  Sales    of Sales
          ------------------------------------------------------------------
          Northeast Alomar   $786.00      12%
                    Andrews  $1,045.00    17%  Sales substantially
                                               above expectations.

          Northwest Brown    $598.00       9%
                    Pelfrey  $746.00      12%
                    Reveiz   $1,110.00    18%  Sales substantially
                                               above expectations.

          Southeast Jones    $630.00      10%
                    Smith    $350.00       6%
          Southwest Adams    $695.00      11%
                    Taylor   $353.00       6%
                             ---------   ---------
                             $6,313.00    100%
```

The COLUMN statement uses the text in quotation marks as a spanning header. The header spans all the columns in the report because they are all included in the pair of parentheses that contains the header.

```
options nodate nonumber fmtsearch=(sasuser);
  proc report data=sasuser.grocery nowd headline ls=70 ps=18;
     title;
     column ('Individual Store Sales as a Percent of All Sales'
             sector manager sales,(sum pctsum) comment);
     define manager/group format=$mgrfmt. 'Manager';
     define sector/group format=$sctrfmt. 'Sector';
     define sales / format=dollar11.2 '';
     define sum / 'Total Sales' format=dollar9.2 ;
```

The COLUMN statement associates two statistics with SALES: SUM and PCTSUM. The SUM statistic sums the values of SALES for all observations included in a row of the report. THE PCTSUM statistic shows what percentage that sum is of SALES for all observations in the report.

The DEFINE statement for PCTSUM specifies a column header, a format, and a column width of 8. The PERCENT. format presents the value of PCTSUM as a percentage rather than a decimal.

```
define pctsum / 'Percent of Sales' format=percent6. width=8;
define comment / computed
                 width=25 ''
                 flow;
```

The DEFINE statement for COMMENT defines it as a computed variable and assigns it a column width of 25 and a blank column header. The FLOW option wraps the text for COMMENT onto multiple lines if it exceeds the column width.

Options in the COMPUTE statement define COMMENT as a character variable with a length of 40.

```
compute comment  / char length=40;
```

*When you create a compute block for a variable, PROC REPORT executes that compute block on each line of the report. This compute block creates a comment that says "Sales substantially above expectations." for every store where sales exceeded 15% of the sales for all stores. Of course, on the summary row for the report, the value of PCTSUM is 100. However, it is inappropriate to flag this row as having exceptional sales. In this report, you can identify the summary row because it is the only row that contains a missing value for MANAGER.*

**Note:**  *This technique depends on there being no missing values for MANAGER in the input data set.*

```
         if sales.pctsum gt .15 and manager ne ' '
            then comment='Sales substantially above expectations.';
         else comment=' ';
      endcomp;
      rbreak after / ol summarize;
run;
```

# Example 11

This example illustrates the difference between the way PROC REPORT handles missing values for group (or order or across) variables with and without the MISSING option.

*Report That Does Not Include Missing Values*

```
          SECTOR    MANAGER        N      SALES
          ----------------------------------------
          Northeast Alomar         3    $596.00
                    Andrews        4  $1,045.00
          Northwest Brown          4    $598.00
                    Pelfrey        4    $746.00
                    Reveiz         3    $690.00
          Southeast Jones          4    $630.00
                    Smith          2    $130.00
          Southwest Adams          3    $655.00
                    Taylor         4    $353.00
                             =========  =========
                                 31  $5,443.00
```

*Report That Does Include*
*Missing Values*

```
              SECTOR    MANAGER      N     SALES
         -----------------------------------------
                                     1     $40.00
                         Reveiz      1    $420.00
                         Smith       1    $100.00
              Northeast              1    $190.00
                         Alomar      3    $596.00
                         Andrews     4  $1,045.00
              Northwest  Brown       4    $598.00
                         Pelfrey     4    $746.00
                         Reveiz      3    $690.00
              Southeast              1    $120.00
                         Jones       4    $630.00
                         Smith       2    $130.00
              Southwest  Adams       3    $655.00
                         Taylor      4    $353.00
                                 ========= =========
                                    36  $6,313.00
```

*SASUSER.GROCMISS is*
*identical to SASUSER.GROCERY*
*except that it contains some*
*observations with missing values*
*for SECTOR, MANAGER, or*
*both.*

```
data sasuser.grocmiss;
    input sector $ manager $ dept $ sales @@;
cards;
se 1 np1 50     .  1 p1 100    se . np2 120    se 1 p2 80
se 2 np1 40    se 2 p1 300    se 2 np2 220    se 2 p2 70
nw 3 np1 60    nw 3 p1 600     .  3 np2 420    nw 3 p2 30
nw 4 np1 45    nw 4 p1 250    nw 4 np2 230    nw 4 p2 73
nw 9 np1 45    nw 9 p1 205    nw 9 np2 420    nw 9 p2 76
sw 5 np1 53    sw 5 p1 130    sw 5 np2 120    sw 5 p2 50
 .  . np1 40    sw 6 p1 350    sw 6 np2 225    sw 6 p2 80
ne 7 np1 90    ne . p1 190    ne 7 np2 420    ne 7 p2 86
ne 8 np1 200   ne 8 p1 300    ne 8 np2 420    ne 8 p2 125
;
```

*In this example, SECTOR and*
*MANAGER are group variables.*
*In this PROC REPORT step, the*
*procedure does not include*
*observations with a missing value*
*for the group variable.*

```
title;
options nodate nonumber ps=18 ls=70 fmtsearch=(sasuser);
proc report data=sasuser.grocmiss nowd headline;
    column sector manager n sales;
    define sector/group format=$sctrfmt.;
    define manager/group format=$mgrfmt.;
    define sales/ format=dollar9.2;
    rbreak after/dol summarize;
run;
```

*The MISSING option in the*
*second PROC REPORT step*
*includes these observations. The*
*differences in the reports are*
*apparent if you compare the*
*values of N for each row and*
*compare the totals in the default*
*summary at the end of the report.*

```
proc report data=sasuser.grocmiss nowd headline missing;
    column sector manager n sales;
    define sector/group format=$sctrfmt.;
    define manager/group format=$mgrfmt.;
    define sales/ format=dollar9.2;
    rbreak after/dol summarize;
run;
```

# Example 12

This example uses WHERE processing as it builds an output data set. This technique allows you to do WHERE processing after you have consolidated multiple observations into a single row.

The first PROC REPORT step creates a report (which it does not display) in which each row represents all the observations from the input data set for a single manager. The WHERE= data set option on the OUT= option filters those rows as PROC REPORT creates the output data set. Only those observations with sales that exceed $1,000 become observations in the output data set. The second PROC REPORT step builds a report from the output data set.

*This is the final report.*

```
                         The SAS System

                    ............................
                    |MANAGER         SALES|
                    ---------------------
                    |Andrews|    $1,045.00|
                    --------+------------
                    |Reveiz |    $1,110.00|
                    ---------------------
```

*This is the output data set created by the first PROC REPORT step. It is used as input for the final report.*

```
                         The SAS System

            MANAGER         SALES   _BREAK__
                3            1110
                8            1045
```

*OUT= creates the output data set SASUSER.TEMP. The output data set contains a variable for each column in the report (MANAGER and SALES) as well as the variable _BREAK_, which is not used in this example. Each observation in the data set represents a row of the report.*

*Because MANAGER is a group variable and SALES is an analysis variable used to calculate the SUM statistic, each row in the report (and therefore each observation in the output data set) represents multiple observations from the input data set. In particular, each value of SALES in the output data set is the total of all values of SALES for that manager.*

*The WHERE= data set option on the OUT= option filters those rows as PROC REPORT creates the output data set. Only those observations with sales that exceed $1,000 become observations in the output data set.*

```
options nodate nonumber ps=18 ls=70 fmtsearch=(sasuser);
proc report data=sasuser.grocery nowd
            out=sasuser.temp( where=(sales gt 1000 ));
    column manager sales;
```

*Because the definitions of all report items in this report include the NOPRINT option, PROC REPORT does not print a report. However, the PROC REPORT step does execute and create an output data set.*

```
    define manager / group noprint;
    define sales / analysis sum noprint;
run;
```

*DATA= specifies the output data set from the previous PROC REPORT step as the input data set for this report. The BOX option draws an outline around the output, separates the column headers from the body of the report, and separates rows and columns of data.*

```
proc report data=sasuser.temp box nowd;
    column  manager sales;
    define manager / group format=$mgrfmt.;
    define sales / analysis sum format=dollar11.2;
    title 'Managers with Daily Sales of over One Thousand Dollars';
run;
```

# Example 13

This report creates a computed variable, stores it in an output data set, and uses that data set to create a chart based on the computed variable.

*This is the output data set created by the PROC REPORT step. It is used as input for PROC CHART.*

| Sector | Manager | DEPT | Sales | Profit | _BREAK_ |
|--------|---------|------|-------|--------|---------|
| ne | 7 | np1 | 90 | 36 | |
| ne | 7 | np2 | 420 | 168 | |
| ne | 7 | p1 | 190 | 47.5 | |
| ne | 7 | p2 | 86 | 21.5 | |
| ne | 8 | np1 | 200 | 80 | |
| ne | 8 | np2 | 420 | 168 | |
| ne | 8 | p1 | 300 | 75 | |
| ne | 8 | p2 | 125 | 31.25 | |
| nw | 4 | np1 | 45 | 18 | |
| nw | 4 | np2 | 230 | 92 | |
| nw | 4 | p1 | 250 | 62.5 | |
| nw | 4 | p2 | 73 | 18.25 | |
| nw | 9 | np1 | 45 | 18 | |
| nw | 9 | np2 | 420 | 168 | |
| nw | 9 | p1 | 205 | 51.25 | |
| nw | 9 | p2 | 76 | 19 | |
| nw | 3 | np1 | 60 | 24 | |
| nw | 3 | np2 | 420 | 168 | |
| nw | 3 | p1 | 600 | 150 | |
| nw | 3 | p2 | 30 | 7.5 | |
| se | 2 | np1 | 40 | 16 | |
| se | 2 | np2 | 220 | 88 | |
| se | 2 | p1 | 300 | 75 | |
| se | 2 | p2 | 70 | 17.5 | |
| se | 1 | np1 | 50 | 20 | |
| se | 1 | np2 | 120 | 48 | |
| se | 1 | p1 | 100 | 25 | |
| se | 1 | p2 | 80 | 20 | |
| sw | 6 | np1 | 40 | 16 | |
| sw | 6 | np2 | 225 | 90 | |
| sw | 6 | p1 | 350 | 87.5 | |
| sw | 6 | p2 | 80 | 20 | |
| sw | 5 | np1 | 53 | 21.2 | |
| sw | 5 | np2 | 120 | 48 | |
| sw | 5 | p1 | 130 | 32.5 | |
| sw | 5 | p2 | 50 | 12.5 | |

*This is the chart created from the output data set.*

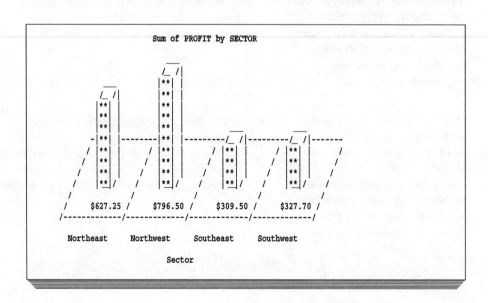

*OUT= creates the output data set SASUSER.PROFIT. This data set contains a variable for each column in the report, including PROFIT, which is not in the original input data set.*

```
options nodate pageno=1 ps=60 ls=66 fmtsearch=(sasuser);
   title;
   proc report data=sasuser.grocery nowd out=sasuser.profit;
      column sector manager dept sales profit;
      define sector / 'Sector'  group format=$sctrfmt.;
      define manager / 'Manager' group format=$mgrfmt.;
      define profit / 'Profit' computed format=dollar11.2;
      define sales / 'Sales' analysis sum format=dollar11.2;
      define dept / group ;
      /* Compute values for PROFIT. */
      compute profit;
         if dept='np1' or dept='np2' then profit=0.4*sales.sum;
         else profit=0.25*sales.sum;
      endcomp;
   run;
```

*PROC CHART uses the output data set from the previous PROC REPORT step to chart the sum of PROFIT for each sector.*

```
proc chart data=sasuser.profit;
   block sector / sumvar=profit;
   format sector $sctrfmt.;
   format profit dollar7.2;
run;
```

# CHAPTER *4* **PROC REPORT Windows**

*BREAK* **78**
*Path* **78**
*Description* **78**
  *Color* **81**
  *Pushbuttons* **81**
*COMPUTE* **81**
*Path* **81**
*Description* **81**
*COMPUTED VAR* **81**
*Path* **81**
*Description* **82**
*DATA COLUMNS* **82**
*Path* **82**
*Description* **82**
*DATA SELECTION* **83**
*Path* **83**
*Description* **83**
  *Pushbuttons* **83**
*DEFINITION* **83**
*Path* **83**
*Description* **84**
  *Usage* **84**
  *Attributes* **84**
  *Options* **87**
  *Color* **88**
  *Pushbuttons* **88**
*DISPLAY PAGE* **88**
*Path* **88**
*Description* **88**
*EXPLORE* **88**
*Path* **89**
*Description* **89**
  *Pushbuttons* **89**
*LAYOUT* **90**
*Path* **90**
*Description* **90**
  *Pushbuttons* **90**
  *Navigating in the LAYOUT Window* **90**
  *Altering the Layout of Existing Report Items* **91**
  *Changing Report Item Definitions* **91**
  *Adding and Deleting a Report Item* **91**
  *Adding, Altering, and Deleting Default Summaries* **92**
  *Adding and Deleting Customized Summaries* **92**
  *Changing Settings in the ROPTIONS Window* **93**
  *Limiting the Number of Observations Displayed* **94**
*LOAD REPORT* **94**
*Path* **94**
*Description* **94**
  *Pushbuttons* **94**
*MESSAGE* **95**
*PROFILE* **95**
*Path* **95**
*Description* **95**
  *Pushbuttons* **95**
*PROMPTER* **96**
*Path* **96**
*Description* **96**
  *Pushbuttons* **96**

*REPORT*  **96**
*Path*  **96**
*Description*  **96**
*REPORT DATA*  **97**
*Path*  **97**
*ROPTIONS*  **97**
*Path*  **97**
*Description*  **97**
  *Modes*  **97**
  *Options*  **97**
  *Attributes*  **99**
  *Pushbuttons*  **101**
*RSTORE*  **101**
*Path*  **101**
*Description*  **101**
*STATISTIC*  **101**
*Path*  **101**
*Description*  **101**

## BREAK

**Controls PROC REPORT's actions at a change in the value of a group or order variable or at the top or bottom of a report.**

## Path

After you select Summarize information, PROC REPORT offers you four choices for the location of the break:

□ Before detail lines

□ After detail lines

□ At top of report

□ At bottom of report

After you select a location, the BREAK window opens.

   **Note:**  To create a break before or after detail lines (when the value of a group or order variable changes), you must select a variable before you open the BREAK window.

## Description

```
+-------------SAS: BREAK---------------------+
|         <Information identifying break>    |
|Options                            Color    |
|_ Overline summary                 BLUE     |
|_ Double overline summary          RED      |
|_ Underline summary                PINK     |
|_ Double underline summary         GREEN    |
|                                   CYAN     |
|_ Skip line after break            YELLOW   |
|_ Page after break                 WHITE    |
|                                   ORANGE   |
|_ Summarize analysis columns     * BLACK    |
|_ Suppress break value             MAGENTA  |
|                                   GRAY     |
|                                   BROWN    |
|                                            |
| Edit Program      OK      Cancel           |
+--------------------------------------------+
```

**Note:** For information on changing the system form characters used by the line drawing options in this window, see "Using Form Characters" in Chapter 2.

Overline summary
> uses the second system form character to overline each value

> □ that appears in the summary line

> □ that would appear in the summary line if you specified the SUMMARIZE option.

> Default: -
> Interaction: If you specify options to overline and to double overline, PROC REPORT overlines.

Double overline summary
> uses the thirteenth system form character to overline each value

> □ that appears in the summary line

> □ that would appear in the summary line if you specified the SUMMARIZE option.

> Default: =
> Interaction: If you specify options to overline and to double overline, PROC REPORT overlines.

Underline summary
> uses the second system form character to underline each value

> □ that appears in the summary line

> □ that would appear in the summary line if you specified the SUMMARIZE option.

> Default: -
> Interaction: If you specify options to underline and to double underline, PROC REPORT underlines.

Double underline summary
> uses the thirteenth system form character to overline each value

> □ that appears in the summary line

> □ that would appear in the summary line if you specified the SUMMARIZE option.

> Default: =
> Interaction: If you specify options to overline and to double overline, PROC REPORT overlines.

Skip line after break
> writes a blank line for the last break line.
> This option has no affect if you use it in a break at the end of a report.

Page after break
> starts a new page after the last break line. This option has no effect in a break at the end of a report.

> Interaction: If you use this option in a break on a variable and you create a break at the end of the report, the summary for the whole report is on a separate page.

Summarize analysis columns

writes a summary line in each group of break lines. A summary line contains values for

□ statistics

□ analysis variables

□ computed variables.

A summary line between sets of observations also contains:

□ the break variable (which you can suppress with SUPPRESS)

□ other group or order variables to the left of the break variable.

The following table shows how PROC REPORT calculates the value for each kind of report item in a summary line created by the BREAK window:

| If the report item is ... | then its value is ... |
|---|---|
| the break variable | the current value of the variable (or a missing value if you use **Suppress break value**) |
| a group or order variable to the left of the break variable | the current value of the variable |
| a group or order variable to the right of the break variable, or a display variable anywhere in the report | missing* |
| a statistic | the value of the statistic over all observations in the set |
| an analysis variable | the value of the statistic specified as the usage option in the item's definition. PROC REPORT calculates the value of the statistic over all observations in the set. The default usage is SUM. |
| a computed variable | the results of the calculations based on the code in the corresponding compute block (see "COMPUTE Statement"). |

*If you reference a variable with a missing value in a customized summary line, PROC REPORT displays a blank (for character variables) or a period (for numeric variables).

Suppress break value

suppresses printing of

□ the value of the break variable in the summary line

□ any underlining and overlining in the break lines in the column containing the break variable.

If you use **Suppress break value**, the value of the break variable is unavailable for use in customized break lines unless you assign it a value in the compute block associated with the break.

## Color

From the list of colors, select the one to use for the column header and the values of the item that you are defining.

Default:   The color of "Foreground" in the SASCOLOR window. (See "SAS Global Color and Attribute Settings" in Chapter 1 of *SAS Software: Changes and Enhancements, Release 6.10*).

Note:   Not all operating systems and devices support all colors, and on some operating systems and devices, one color may map to another color. For example, if the DEFINITION window displays BROWN in yellow characters, selecting BROWN results in a yellow item.

## Pushbuttons

Edit Program
> opens the COMPUTE window and lets you associate a compute block with a location in the report.

OK
> applies the information in the BREAK window to the report and closes the window.

Cancel
> closes the BREAK window without applying information to the report.

---

## COMPUTE

**Attaches a compute block to a report item or to a location in the report. Use the SAS text editor commands to manipulate text in this window.**

### Path

From Edit Program in the COMPUTED VAR, DEFINITION, or BREAK window.

### Description

For information on the SAS language features that you can use in the COMPUTE window, see "The Contents of Compute Blocks" on page 12.

---

## COMPUTED VAR

**Adds a variable that is not in the input data set to the report.**

### Path

Select a column. Then select

After you select Computed column, PROC REPORT offers you the choice of placing the computed variable

□  at right of selected item

□  at left of selected item

□  above selected item

□  below selected item

After you select a location, the COMPUTED VAR window opens.

## Description

Enter the name of the variable at the prompt. If it is a character variable, select the "Character data" check box and, if you want, enter a value in the "Length" field. The length can be any integer between 1 and 200. If you leave the field blank, PROC REPORT assigns a length of 8 to the variable.

After you enter the name of the variable, select $\boxed{\text{Edit Program}}$ to open the COMPUTE window. Use programming statements in the COMPUTE window to define the computed variable. After closing the COMPUTE and COMPUTED VAR windows, open the DEFINITION window to describe how to display the computed variable.

▶ **Caution:** *Postion of Computed Variables*

Because PROC REPORT assigns values to the columns in a row of a report from left to right, a computed variable can depend only on values to its left.

. . . . . . . . . . . . . . . . . . . . . . . . . . . . . . . . . . . . . . . . . . . . . . . . . . . . . . . . . . . . . . . .

## DATA COLUMNS

**Lists all variables in the input data set so that you can add one or more data set variables to the report.**

## Path

Select a report item. Then select

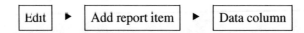

$\boxed{\text{Edit}}$ ▶ $\boxed{\text{Add report item}}$ ▶ $\boxed{\text{Data column}}$

After you select $\boxed{\text{Data column}}$, PROC REPORT offers you the choice of placing the variable

□ at right of selected item

□ at left of selected item

□ above selected item

□ below selected item

After you select a location, the DATA COLUMNS window opens.

## Description

Select one or more variables to add to the report. When you select the first variable, it moves to the top of the list in the window. If you select multiple variables, subsequent selections move to the bottom of the list of selected variables. An asterisk (*) identifies each selected variable. The order of selected variables from top to bottom determines their order in the report from left to right.

## DATA SELECTION

**Loads a data set into the current report definition.**

▶ *Caution:* *Use Data Compatible with the Current Report Definition*

## Path

## Description

The first list box in the DATA SELECTION window lists all the librefs defined for your SAS session. The second one lists all the SAS data sets in the selected library.

The data set that you load must contain variables whose names are the same as the variable names in the current report definition.

. . . . . . . . . . . . . . . . . . . . . . . . . . . . . . . . . . . . . . . . . . . . . . . . . . . . .

## Pushbuttons

[OK]
loads the selected data set into the current report definition.

[Cancel]
closes the DATA SELECTION window without loading new data.

## DEFINITION

**Displays the characteristics associated with an item in the report and lets you change them.**

## Path

**OR**

Double-click the selected item. (Not all operating systems support this method of opening the DEFINITION window.)

## Description

```
+------------------- SAS: DEFINITION ---------------------------+
|                  Definition of _____                      |
|  Usage    Attributes                 Options        Color    |
|_ DISPLAY   Format    = _____     _ NOPRINT      BLUE      |
|_ ORDER     Spacing   = _____     _ NOZERO       RED       |
|_ GROUP     Width     = _____     _ DESCENDING   PINK      |
|_ ACROSS    Item Help = _____     _ PAGE         GREEN     |
|_ ANALYSIS  Statistic = _____     _ FLOW         CYAN      |
|_ COMPUTED  Order     = _____     _ ID column    YELLOW    |
|            Justify   = _____                    WHITE     |
|            Data type = _____                    ORANGE    |
|            Alias     = _____                  * BLACK     |
|                                                    MAGENTA   |
|                                                    GRAY      |
| Header =                                           BROWN     |
|     Apply    Edit Program    OK    Cancel                    |
+--------------------------------------------------------------+
```

## Usage

For an explanation of each type of usage see "Report Layout" in Chapter 2.

DISPLAY
  defines the selected item as a display variable.

ORDER
  defines the selected item as an order variable.

GROUP
  defines the selected item as a group variable.

ACROSS
  defines the selected item as an across variable.

ANALYSIS
  defines the selected item as an analysis variable. You must specify a statistic (see "Attributes") for an analysis variable.

COMPUTED
  defines the selected item as a computed variable. Computed variables are variables that you define for the report. They are not in the input data set, and PROC REPORT does not add them to the input data set. However, computed variables are included in an output data set if you create one.
  In the windowing environment, you add a computed variable to a report from the COMPUTED VAR window.

## Attributes

Format =
  assigns a SAS or user-defined format to the item. This format applies to the selected item as PROC REPORT displays it; the format does not alter the format associated with a variable in the data set. For data set variables, PROC REPORT honors the first of these formats that it finds:

  1. the format assigned with FORMAT= in the DEFINITION statement
  2. the format assigned in a FORMAT statement when you start PROC REPORT
  3. the format associated with the variable in the data set.

If none of these is present, PROC REPORT uses BEST*w.* for numeric variables and $w. for character variables. The value of *w* is the default column width. For character variables in the input data set, the default column width is the variable's length. For numeric variables in the input data set and for computed variables (both numeric and character), the default column width is the value of the COLWIDTH= option in the PROC REPORT statement.

If you are unsure what format to use, type a question mark (?) in the format field in the DEFINITION window to access the FORMATS window.

Spacing =

defines the number of blank characters to leave between the column being defined and the column immediately to its left. For each column, the sum of its width and the blank characters between it and the column to its left cannot exceed the line size.

Default: 2

Interaction: When PROC REPORT's CENTER option is in effect, PROC REPORT ignores spacing that precedes the leftmost variable in the report.

Interaction: SPACING= in an item definition overrides the value of SPACING= in the PROC REPORT statement or the ROPTIONS window.

Width =

defines the width of the column in which PROC REPORT displays the selected item.

Range: 1 to the value of the LINESIZE= system option

Default: A column width that is just large enough to handle the format. If there is no format, PROC REPORT uses the value of COLWIDTH=.

**Note:** When you stack items in the same column in a report, the width of the item that is at the bottom of the stack determines the width of the column.

Item Help =

references a HELP or CBT entry that contains help information for the selected item. Use PROC BUILD in SAS/AF Software to create a HELP or CBT entry for a report item. All HELP and CBT entries for a report must be in the same catalog, and you must specify that catalog with the HELP= option in the PROC REPORT statement or from the User Help fields in the ROPTIONS window.

To access a help entry from the report, select the item and issue the HELP command. PROC REPORT first searches for and displays an entry named *entry-name*.CBT. If no such entry exists, it searches for *entry-name*.HELP. If neither a CBT nor a HELP entry for the selected item exists, the opening frame of the help for PROC REPORT is displayed.

Statistic =

associates a statistic with an analysis variable. You must associate a statistic with every analysis variable in its definition. PROC REPORT uses the statistic you specify to calculate values for the analysis variable for the observations represented by each cell of the report. You cannot use *statistic* in the definition of any other kind of variable.

Default: SUM

**Note:** PROC REPORT uses the name of the analysis variable as the default header for the column. You can customize the column header with the "Header" field of the DEFINITION window.

You can use the following values for *statistic* :

| N | RANGE | T |
| NMISS | SUM | PRT |
| MEAN | USS | VAR |
| STD | CSS | SUMWGT |
| MIN | STDERR | PCTN |
| MAX | CV | PCTSUM |

More:      For definitions of these statistics, see "Statistics Available in PROC REPORT" in Chapter 2.

**Order =**

orders the values of a GROUP, ORDER, or ACROSS variable according to the specified order, where

DATA               orders values according to their order in the input data set.

FORMATTED    orders values by their formatted (external) values. By default, the order is ascending.

FREQ              orders values by ascending frequency count.

INTERNAL     orders values by the same sequence as PROC SORT would use. This sort sequence is particularly useful for displaying dates chronologically.

Default:       FORMATTED

Interaction:    DESCENDING in the item's definition reverses the sort sequence for an item.

▶ **Caution:** *Default for the ORDER= Option*

In other SAS procedures, the default is ORDER=INTERNAL. The default for the option in PROC REPORT may change in a future release to be consistent with other procedures. Therefore, in production jobs where it is important to order report items by their formatted values, specify ORDER=FORMATTED even though it is currently the default. Doing so ensures that PROC REPORT will continue to produce the reports you expect even if the default changes.

. . . . . . . . . . . . . . . . . . . . . . . . . . . . . . . . . . . . . . . . . . . . . . . . . . .

**Justify =**

You can justify the placement of the column header and of the values of the item that you are defining within a column in one of three ways:

LEFT       left-justifies the formatted values of the item that you are defining within the column width and left-justifies the column header over the values. If the format width is the same as the width of the column, LEFT has no effect on the placement of values.

RIGHT     right-justifies the formatted values of the item that you are defining within the column width and right-justifies the column header over the values. If the format width is the same as the width of the column, RIGHT has no effect on the placement of values.

CENTER    centers the formatted values of the item that you are defining within the column width and centers the column header over the values. This option has no effect on the setting of the SAS system option CENTER.

When justifying values, PROC REPORT justifies the field width defined by the format of the item within the column. Thus, numbers are always aligned.

Data type =
>   shows you if the report item is numeric or character. You cannot change this field.

Alias =
>   By entering a name in the "Alias" field, you create an alias for the report item that you are defining. Aliases let you distinguish between different uses of the same report item.
>
>   When you refer in a compute block to a report item that has an alias, you must use the alias (see Example 3 in Chapter 3).

## Options

NOPRINT
>   suppresses the display of the item that you are defining. Use this option
>
>   □ if you do not want to show the item in the report but you need to use the values in it to calculate other values you use in the report
>
>   □ to establish the order of rows in the report
>
>   □ if you do not want to use the item as a column but want to have access to its values in summaries (see Example 9).
>
>   Interaction:    SHOWALL in the PROC REPORT statement or the ROPTIONS window overrides all occurrences of NOPRINT.

NOZERO
>   suppresses the display of the item that you are defining if its values are all zero or missing.
>
>   Interaction:    SHOWALL option in the PROC REPORT statement or the ROPTIONS window overrides all occurrences of NOZERO.

DESCENDING
>   reverses the order in which PROC REPORT displays rows or values of a group, order, or across variable.

PAGE
>   inserts a page break just before printing the first column containing values of the selected item.
>
>   Interaction:    PAGE is ignored if you use WRAP in the PROC REPORT statement or the ROPTIONS window.

FLOW
>   wraps the value of a character variable in its column. The FLOW option honors the split character. If the text contains no split character, PROC REPORT tries to split text at a blank.

ID column
>   specifies that the item that you are defining is an ID variable. An ID variable and all columns to its left appear at the left of every page of a report. ID ensures that you can identify each row of the report when the report contains more columns than will fit on one page.

## Color

From the list of colors, select the one to use for the column header and the values of
the item that you are defining.

Default:     The color of "Foreground" in the SASCOLOR window (see "SAS
             Global Color and Attribute Settings" in Chapter 1 of *SAS Software:
             Changes and Enhancements, Release 6.10*).

Note:        Not all operating systems and devices support all colors, and on some
             operating systems and devices, one color may map to another color. For
             example, if the DEFINITION window displays BROWN in yellow
             characters, selecting BROWN results in a yellow item.

## Pushbuttons

Apply
> applies the information in the open window to the report and keeps the window
> open.

Edit Program
> opens the COMPUTE window and lets you associate a compute block with the
> variable that you are defining.

OK
> applies the information in the DEFINITION window to the report and closes the
> window.

Cancel
> closes the DEFINITION window without applying information to the report.

---

# DISPLAY PAGE

**Lets you view a particular page
of the report.**

## Path

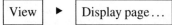

## Description

You can get to the last page of the report by entering a large number for the page
number. When you are on the last page of the report, PROC REPORT sends a note
to the message line of the REPORT window.

---

# EXPLORE

**Lets you experiment with your
data.**

In the EXPLORE window you can

□ subset the data with list boxes

□ suppress the display of a column with the "Remove Column" checkbox

□ change the order of the columns with Rotate columns .

## Path

## Description

You cannot open the EXPLORE window unless your report contains at least one group or order variable.

**Note:** The results of your manipulations in the EXPLORE window appear in the REPORT window but are not saved in report definitions.

list boxes

The EXPLORE window contains three list boxes. These boxes contain the value "All levels" as well as actual values for the first three group or order variables in your report. The values reflect any WHERE clause processing that is in effect. For example, if you use a WHERE clause to subset the data so that it includes only the northeast and northwest sectors, the only values that appear in the list box for SECTOR are "All levels", "Northeast", and "Northwest". Selecting "All levels" in this case displays rows of the report for only the northeast and northwest sectors. To see data for all the sectors, you must clear the WHERE clause before you open the EXPLORE window.

Selecting values in the list boxes restricts the display in the REPORT window to the values that you select. If you select incompatible values, PROC REPORT returns an error.

Remove Column

Above each list box in the EXPLORE window is a check box labeled "Remove Column". Selecting this check box and applying the change removes the column from the REPORT window. You can easily restore the column by clearing the check box and applying that change.

## Pushbuttons

OK
applies the information in the EXPLORE window to the report and closes the window.

Apply
applies the information in the EXPLORE window to the report and keeps the window open.

Rotate columns
changes the order of the variables displayed in the list boxes. Each variable that can move one column to the left does; the leftmost variable moves to the third column.

Cancel
closes the EXPLORE window without applying information to the report.

## LAYOUT

**Provides a template of the report. You can use drag and drop techniques in the template to alter the layout of the report. You can also modify definitions, summaries, and report options.**

## Path

## Description

The LAYOUT window consists of one or more areas that represent parts of the report. The first area contains rectangles that represent report items and spanning headers. Other areas contain information describing the summaries in the report. Rectangles in a summary area represent text and variables in the summary.

From the LAYOUT window you can

□ alter the layout of existing report items

□ change item definitions

□ add and delete report items

□ add, alter, and delete summaries

□ change settings in the ROPTIONS window

□ limit the number of observations displayed in the report.

## Pushbuttons

OK
applies the information in the LAYOUT window to the report and closes the window.

Apply
applies the information in the LAYOUT window to the report and leaves the window open.

Cancel
closes the LAYOUT window without applying changes made with Apply .

## Navigating in the LAYOUT Window

The following table shows how to work with items in the LAYOUT window.

| Task | Process |
|---|---|
| Select an area or a rectangle | Position the mouse pointer over it and press mouse button 1 (MB1). |
| Clear an area or rectangle | Move the pointer off it and press MB1. |
| Move an item | Select the rectangle that represents it and drag it to a new location in its area. |
| Resize a rectangle | Place the pointer near a vertical edge and drag the edge to the desired location. |
| Delete an item | Move its rectangle outside of its area. Or, with the item selected, select Edit → Delete . |
| Apply changes made in the LAYOUT window to the report | Select Apply (to leave the window open) or OK (to close the window). |

| Task | Process |
|---|---|
| Change the size of the LAYOUT window | Select Edit → Zoom layout. This command toggles the size of the LAYOUT window between its original size and its maximum size. |

To group multiple rectangles so that you can treat them as one item

1. position the pointer above or below a rectangle
2. press and hold down MB1
3. move the pointer down or up into the rectangle
4. slide the pointer through all the items that you want in the group
5. release MB1.

**Note:** Whenever the documentation for the LAYOUT window says that you can open a window by double-clicking, it provides an alternate method. If your operating system does not support this capability, use the alternative.

## Altering the Layout of Existing Report Items

The report layout area contains a rectangle for each item and each spanning header in the report. The positions of the rectangles in the report layout area reflect the positions of the corresponding items in the report. If you move the rectangles and apply the changes, the report changes.

**Note:** Moving and resizing the rectangles enable you to visualize how you want the report to look. Resizing is essential if you need to show stacked variables. For instance, the rectangle for an analysis variable that has three statistics under it must span the rectangles of all three statistics. However, moving or resizing an item has no effect on its definition. If you move the rectangles into an arrangement that is not supported by the corresponding definitions, PROC REPORT returns an error when you apply the changes.

## Changing Report Item Definitions

Open the DEFINITION window for a report item either by double-clicking on the item or, with the item selected, by selecting

To apply changes from the DEFINITION window, select either Apply or OK in the DEFINITION window. Apply makes the changes in the REPORT window and leaves the DEFINITION window open. OK closes the DEFINITION window without immediately altering the REPORT window. To see the changes that you specified, select Apply in the LAYOUT window.

## Adding and Deleting a Report Item

To add a report item to the report, select

Select the kind of item that you want to add, and make the appropriate choices in the window that opens.

To delete a report item, drag its rectangle out of the layout area. Or, with the item selected, select Edit → Delete .

## Adding, Altering, and Deleting Default Summaries

To add a default summary from the LAYOUT window

1. Select

2. Select the kind of summary that you want to add.
3. If appropriate, select a break variable from the REPORT COLUMNS window and close that window.

When PROC REPORT creates a summary from the LAYOUT window, it selects the options to use based on the location of the report. Options always include "Summarize analysis columns."

To alter an existing default summary, change the options in the BREAK window for that summary:

1. Select the area containing the summary that you want to modify.
2. Open the BREAK window for that summary by either double-clicking in the summary area or, with the summary selected, selecting

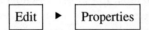

3. Make the appropriate changes in the BREAK window.
    To apply changes from the BREAK window, select OK , which closes the BREAK window. To see the changes that you specified, select Apply in the LAYOUT window.

    To customize a default summary by adding text, variable values, or both, see "Adding and Deleting Customized Summaries".

To delete a summary, select it and select

## Adding and Deleting Customized Summaries

To create a customized summary, you must first create a default summary (see "Adding, Altering, and Deleting Default Summaries"). Once the default summary is in place, you can customize it by adding text, variable values, or both. You may also want to remove the default summary while leaving the customized summary intact by clearing the options in the BREAK window.

  **Note:**    The method described here explains how to use point-and-click methods to customize the summary. If you prefer, you can open the BREAK window associated with the summary, select Edit Program , and write PROC REPORT code directly into the COMPUTE window associated with the break.

To add text to a summary, select

Enter the text in the ADD TEXT window, and select OK. The text appears in the summary area. Select Apply to see the text in the report.

If you want to alter the horizontal placement of the text, open its PROPERTIES window either by double-clicking on the corresponding rectangle in the LAYOUT window, or, with the text selected, by selecting

In the PROPERTIES window for text, you specify a number that adjusts the horizontal position of the text. The number can be a literal value or a variable. If you choose **relative** positioning, the number specifies the number of columns to skip before displaying the first character of the text. If you choose **absolute** positioning, the number specifies the number of the column in which to place the first character of the text.

To add a variable value to a summary, select

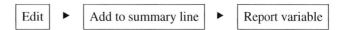

Select one or more variables from the DATA COLUMNS window, and close the window. A rectangle for each variable appears in the summary area.

If you want to alter the format or the horizontal placement of the variable, open its PROPERTIES window either by double-clicking on the corresponding rectangle in the LAYOUT window, or, with the variable selected, by selecting

In the PROPERTIES window for a variable, you specify a format and a number that adjusts the horizontal position of the text. The number can be a literal value or a variable. If you choose **relative** positioning, the number specifies the number of columns to skip before displaying the first character of the text. If you choose **absolute** positioning, the number specifies the number of the column in which to place the first character of the text.

To delete a customized summary, select it and select

## Changing Settings in the ROPTIONS Window

To open the ROPTIONS window, which controls the layout and display of the report as a whole, select the report layout area, but do not select any items in that area. Then, either double-click in the area or select

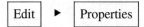

When you select $\boxed{\text{OK}}$ from the ROPTIONS window, the window closes, and PROC REPORT applies the changes to the report.

### Limiting the Number of Observations Displayed

To limit the number of observations displayed in the report, select

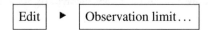

Enter the appropriate number, and select $\boxed{\text{OK}}$ in the Observation Limit... window. Select $\boxed{\text{Apply}}$ in the LAYOUT window.

This limitation remains in effect until you either

□ Apply a new observation limit

□ Close the LAYOUT window.

You can also limit the number of observations if you start PROC REPORT with the PROMPT option or if you select "Search" in the REPORT window. The prompter, like the LAYOUT window, limits observations based on observation number. "Search" limits observations based on WHERE clause criteria.

---

## LOAD REPORT

**Loads a stored report definition.**

## Path

## Description

The first list box in the LOAD REPORT window lists all the librefs defined for your SAS session. The second one lists all the catalogs in the selected library. The third one lists descriptions of all the stored report definitions (entry types of REPT) in the selected catalog. If there is no description for an entry, the list box contains the entry's name.

### Pushbuttons

$\boxed{\text{OK}}$
    loads the current data into the selected report definition.

$\boxed{\text{Cancel}}$
    closes the LOAD REPORT window without loading a new report definition.

**Note:**   Issuing the END command in the REPORT window returns you to the previous report definition (with the current data).

## MESSAGE

**Automatically opens to display notes, warnings, and errors returned by PROC REPORT.**

You must close the MESSAGE window by selecting OK before you can continue to use PROC REPORT.

## PROFILE

**Customizes some features of the PROC REPORT environment.**

The PROFILE window lets you

☐ specify the SAS library, catalog, and entry that define alternative menus to use in the REPORT and COMPUTE windows. Use PROC PMENU to create catalog entries of type PMENU that define these menus. PMENU entries for both windows must be in the same catalog.

☐ set defaults for WINDOWS, PROMPT, and COMMAND. PROC REPORT uses the default option whenever you start the procedure unless you specifically override the option in the PROC REPORT statement.

### Path

### Description

#### Pushbuttons

OK
  stores your profile in SASUSER.PROFILE.REPORT.PROFILE.

Cancel
  closes the window without storing the profile.

## PROMPTER

**Prompts you for information as you add items to a report.**

## Path

Specify the PROMPT option when you start PROC REPORT or select PROMPT from the ROPTIONS window. The PROMPTER window opens the next time that you add an item to the report.

## Description

The prompter guides you through parts of the windows most commonly used to build a report. The title of the window changes to the name of the window you would use to perform a task if you were not using the prompter so that you can begin to associate the windows with their functions and so that you know what window to use if you later decide to change something.

If you start PROC REPORT with prompting, the first window gives you a chance to limit the number of observations used during prompting. When you exit the prompter, PROC REPORT removes the limit.

### Pushbuttons

OK
   applies the information in the open window to the report and continues the prompting process.

Apply
   applies the information in the open window to the report and keeps the window open.

Backup
   returns you to the previous PROMPTER window.

Exit Prompter
   closes the PROMPTER window without applying any more changes to the report. If you have limited the number of observations to use during prompting, PROC REPORT removes the limit.

## REPORT

**Is the surface on which the report appears. You cannot write directly in any part of the REPORT window except column headers. To change other aspects of the report, you select a report item as the target of the next command and issue the command.**

## Path

Use WINDOWS or PROMPT in the PROC REPORT statement.

## Description

To select an item, use a mouse or cursor keys to position the cursor over it. Then click the mouse button or press RETURN.

To execute a command, make a selection from the menu bar at the top of the REPORT window. PROC REPORT displays the effect of a command immediately unless the DEFER option is on.

**Note:**   Issuing the END command in the REPORT window returns you to the previous report definition with the current data. If there is no previous report definition, END closes the REPORT window.

## REPORT DATA

Lets you specify an output data set in which to store the data from the current report.

## Path

---

## ROPTIONS

**Displays choices that control the layout and display of the entire report and identifies the SAS data library and catalog containing CBT or HELP entries for items in the report.**

## Path

## Description

### Modes

DEFER
    stores the information for changes and makes them all at once when you turn DEFER mode off or select

        Edit --> Refresh report display

    DEFER is particularly useful when you know that you need to make several changes to the report but do not want to see the intermediate reports.
        By default, PROC REPORT redisplays the report in the REPORT window each time you redefine the report by adding or deleting an item, by changing information in the DEFINITION window, or by changing information in the BREAK window.

    Interaction:    DEFER has no effect when the LAYOUT window is open.

PROMPT
    opens the PROMPTER window the next time that you add an item to the report.

### Options

CENTER
    centers the report and summary text (customized break lines). If CENTER is not selected, the report is left-justified.
        PROC REPORT honors the first of these centering specifications that it finds:

    □ the CENTER or NOCENTER option in the PROC REPORT statement or the CENTER toggle in the ROPTIONS window

    □ the CENTER or NOCENTER option stored in the report definition loaded with REPORT= in the PROC REPORT statement

    □ the SAS system option CENTER or NOCENTER.

    When PROC REPORT's CENTER option is in effect, PROC REPORT ignores spacing that precedes the leftmost variable in the report.

HEADLINE

    underlines all column headers and the spaces between them at the top of each page of the report.

      HEADLINE underlines with the second system form character.

| | |
|---|---|
| Default: | - |
| Tip: | To underline column headers without underlining the spaces between them, use '—' as the last line of each column header instead of using HEADLINE. |

HEADSKIP

    writes a blank line beneath all column headers (or beneath the underlining that the HEADLINE option writes) at the top of each page of the report.

NAMED

    writes *name=* in front of each value in the report, where *name* is the column header for the value.

| | |
|---|---|
| Tip: | Use NAMED in conjunction with WRAP to produce a report that wraps all columns for a single row of the report onto consecutive lines rather than placing columns of a wide report on separate pages. |
| Interaction: | When you use NAMED, PROC REPORT automatically uses NOHEADER. |

NOHEADER

    suppresses column headers, including those that span multiple columns.

      Once you suppress the display of column headers in the windowing environment, you cannot select any report items.

SHOWALL

    overrides the parts of a definition that suppress the display of a column (NOPRINT and NOZERO). You define a report item with a DEFINE statement or in the DEFINITION window.

WRAP

    displays one value from each column of the report, on consecutive lines if necessary, before displaying another value from the first column. By default, PROC REPORT displays values for only as many columns as it can fit on one page. It fills a page with values for these columns before starting to display values for the remaining columns on the next page.

| | |
|---|---|
| Interaction: | When WRAP is in effect, PROC REPORT ignores PAGE in any item definitions. |
| Tip: | Typically, you use WRAP in conjunction with NAMED to avoid wrapping column headers. |

BOX

    uses the SAS system form characters to add line-drawing characters to the report. These characters

    □ surround each page of the report

    □ separate column headers from the body of the report

    □ separate rows and columns from each other.

| | |
|---|---|
| Interaction: | You cannot use BOX if you use WRAP in the PROC REPORT statement or ROPTIONS window or if you use FLOW in any item's definition. |

MISSING

considers missing values as valid values for group, order, or across variables. Special missing values used to represent numeric values (the letters A through Z and the underscore (_) character) are each considered as a different value. A group for each missing value appears in the report. If you omit the MISSING option, PROC REPORT does not include observations with a missing value for one or more group, order, or across variables in the report.

## Attributes

Linesize

specifies the line size for a report. PROC REPORT honors the first of these linesize specifications that it finds:

□ LS= in the PROC REPORT statement or Linesize= in the ROPTIONS window

□ the LS= setting stored in the report definition loaded with REPORT= in the PROC REPORT statement

□ the SAS system option LINESIZE=.

Range: 64-256 (integer)

Tip: If the linesize is greater than the width of the REPORT window, use the SAS display manager commands RIGHT and LEFT to display portions of the report that are not currently in the display.

Pagesize

specifies the page size for a report. PROC REPORT honors the first of these pagesize specifications that it finds:

□ PS= in the PROC REPORT statement or Pagesize= in the ROPTIONS window

□ the PS= setting stored in the report definition loaded with REPORT= in the PROC REPORT statement

□ the SAS system option PAGESIZE=.

Range: 15-32,767 (integer)

Colwidth

specifies the default number of characters for columns containing computed variables or numeric data set variables.

Range: 1 to the linesize

Default: 9

Interaction: When setting the width for a column, PROC REPORT first looks at WIDTH= in the definition for that column. If WIDTH= is not present, PROC REPORT uses a column width large enough to accommodate the format for the item. (For information on formats, see "Format=" in "DEFINITION Window".)

If no format is associated with the item, the column width depends on variable type:

| If the variable is a ... | then the column width is the ... |
| --- | --- |
| character variable in the input data set | length of the variable |
| numeric variable in the input data set | value of COLWIDTH= option |
| computed variable (numeric or character) | value of COLWIDTH= option |

SPACING=*space-between-columns*
> specifies the number of blank characters between columns. For each column, the sum of its width and the blank characters between it and the column to its left cannot exceed the line size.

> Default: 2
> Interaction: PROC REPORT separates all columns in the report by the number of blank characters specified by SPACING= in the PROC REPORT statement or the ROPTIONS window unless you use SPACING= in the definition of a particular item to change the spacing to the left of that item.
> Interaction: When CENTER is in effect, PROC REPORT ignores spacing that precedes the leftmost variable in the report.

SPLIT='*character*'
> specifies the split character. PROC REPORT breaks a column header when it reaches that character and continues the header on the next line. The split character itself is not part of the column header although each occurrence of the split character counts toward the 40-character maximum for a label.

> Default: /
> Interaction: The FLOW option in the DEFINE statement honors the split character.
> Note: If you are typing over a header (rather than entering one from the PROMPTER or DEFINITION window), you do not see the effect of the split character until you refresh the screen, by adding or deleting an item, by changing the contents of a DEFINITION or a BREAK window, or by selecting

> Edit --> Refresh report display

PANELS=*number-of-panels*
> specifies the number of panels on each page of the report. If the width of a report is less than half of the line size, you can display the data in multiple sets of columns so that rows that would otherwise appear on multiple pages appear on the same page. Each set of columns is a *panel*. A familiar example of this kind of report is a telephone book, which contains multiple panels of names and telephone numbers on a single page.
> When writing a multipanel report, PROC REPORT fills one panel before beginning the next.
> The number of panels that fits on a page depends on the

> □ width of the panel

> □ space between panels

> □ linesize.

> Default: 1
> Tip: If *number-of-panels* is larger than the number of panels that can fit on the page, PROC REPORT creates as many panels as it can. Let PROC REPORT put your data in the maximum number of panels that can fit on the page by specifying a large number of panels (for example, 99).
> See also: For information on the space between panels and the linesize, see the discussions of PSPACE= and LS= in this section.

PSPACE=*space-between-panels*
> specifies the number of blank characters between panels. PROC REPORT separates all panels in the report by the same number of blank characters. For

each panel, the sum of its width and the number of blank characters separating it from the panel to its left cannot exceed the line size.

Default:    4

User Help

identifies the library and catalog containing user-defined help for the report. This help can be in CBT or HELP catalog entries. You can write a CBT or HELP entry for each item in the report with the BUILD procedure in SAS/AF software. You must store all such entries for a report in the same catalog.

Specify the entry name for help for a particular report item in the DEFINITION window for that report item or in a DEFINE statement.

### Pushbuttons

OK

applies the information in the ROPTIONS window to the report and closes the window.

Cancel

closes the ROPTIONS window without applying information to the report.

---

## RSTORE

**Stores a report definition for subsequent use with the same data set or with a similar data set.**

## Path

## Description

The RSTORE window prompts you for the complete name of the catalog entry in which to store the definition of the current report and for an optional description of the report. This description shows up in the LOAD REPORT window and helps you to select the appropriate report.

SAS stores the report definition as a catalog entry of type REPT. You can use a report definition to create an identically structured report for any SAS data set that contains variables with the same names as the ones used in the report definition.

---

## STATISTIC

**Displays statistics that are available in PROC REPORT.**

## Path

## Description

Select the statistics that you want to include in your report and close the window. When you select the first statistic, it moves to the top of the list in the window. If you select multiple statistics, subsequent selections move to the bottom of the list of selected statistics. The order of selected statistics from top to bottom determines their order in the report from left to right.

*Introduction*  **103**
*Sequence of Events*  **103**
   *Compound Names*  **104**
*Building a Report that Uses Groups and a Report Summary*  **105**
*Building a Report that Uses DATA Step Variables*  **109**

CHAPTER *5*  # How PROC REPORT Builds a Report

## Introduction

This chapter first explains the process of building a report. Following this explanation are illustrations of how PROC REPORT creates two sample reports. The examples use programming statements; you can construct the same report in the windowing environment.

To understand the process of building a report, you must understand the difference between report variables and DATA step variables. Variables that appear only in one or more compute blocks are *DATA step variables.* Variables that appear in one or more columns of the report are *report variables.* A report variable may or may not appear in a compute block.

## Sequence of Events

PROC REPORT constructs a report as follows:

1. It consolidates the data by group, order, and across variables. It calculates all statistics for the report, those for detail rows as well as those for summary lines in breaks. Statistics include those computed for analysis variables. PROC REPORT calculates statistics for summary lines whether or not they appear in the report. It stores all this information in a temporary file.
2. It initializes all DATA step variables to missing.
3. It begins constructing the rows of the report.

   a. At the beginning of each row, it initializes all report variables to missing.
   b. It fills in values for report variables from left to right.

      □ Values for computed variables come from executing the statements in the corresponding compute blocks.

      □ Values for all other variables come from the temporary file created at the beginning of the report-building process.

   c. Whenever it comes to a break, PROC REPORT first constructs the break lines created with the BREAK or RBREAK statement or with options in the BREAK window. It then executes the statements in the compute block attached to the break (if there is one).

─────────── Construction of Summary Lines ───────────

PROC REPORT constructs a summary line for a break if either of the following conditions is true:

   □ You summarize numeric variables in the break.

┌─────────────────────────────────────────────────┐
Construction of Summary Lines

□ You use a compute block at the break. (You can attach a compute block to a break without using a BREAK or RBREAK statement or without selecting any options in the BREAK window.)

The summary line that PROC REPORT constructs at this point is preliminary. If no compute block is attached to the break, the preliminary summary line becomes the final summary line. However, if a compute block is attached to the break, the statements in the compute block can alter the values in the preliminary summary line.

PROC REPORT prints the summary line only if you summarize numeric variables in the break.
└─────────────────────────────────────────────────┘

Because of the way PROC REPORT builds a report, you can

□ Use group statistics in compute blocks for a break before the group variable.

□ Use statistics for the whole report in a compute block at the beginning of the report.

This chapter references these statistics with the appropriate compound name. For information on referencing report items in a compute block, see "Four Ways to Reference Report Items in a Compute Block" on page 12.

## Compound Names

When you use a statistic in a report, you generally refer to it in compute blocks by a compound name like SALES.SUM. However, in different parts of the report, that same name takes on different meanings. Consider the report in Output 5.1:

*Output 5.1*
*Three Different Meanings of*
*SALES.SUM.*

```
                    The SAS System                    1

            SECTOR     MANAGER     SALES
            Northeast  Alomar      $786.00
                       Andrews     $1,045.00
            ---------              ---------
            Northeast              $1,831.00

            Northwest  Brown       $598.00
                       Pelfrey     $746.00
                       Reveiz      $1,110.00
            ---------              ---------
            Northwest              $2,454.00

            Southeast  Jones       $630.00
                       Smith       $350.00
            ---------              ---------
            Southeast              $980.00

            Southwest  Adams       $695.00
                       Taylor      $353.00
            ---------              ---------
            Southwest              $1,048.00

            =========              =========
            Total:                 $6,313.00
            =========              =========
```

Here SALES.SUM takes on three different meanings:

□ In detail rows, the value is the sales for one manager's store in a sector of the city. For example, the first detail row of the report shows that the sales for the store that Alomar manages were $786.00.

□ In the group summary lines, the value is the sales for all the stores in one sector. For example, the first group summary line shows that sales for the Northeast sector were $1,831.00.

□ In the report summary line, the value ($6,313.00) is the sales for all stores in the city.

▶ *Caution:*

When you refer in a compute block to a statistic that has an alias, you do not use a compound name. Generally, you must usually use the alias. However, if the statistic shares a column with an across variable, you must reference it by column number (see "Four Ways to Reference Report Items in a Compute Block" on page 12).

. . . . . . . . . . . . . . . . . . . . . . . . . . . . . . . . . . . . . . . . . . . . . . . .

# Building a Report that Uses Groups and a Report Summary

The report in Output 5.2 contains five columns:

□ SECTOR and DEPT are group variables.

□ SALES is an analysis variable used to calculate the SUM statistic.

□ PROFIT is a computed variable based on the value of DEPT.

□ The N statistic indicates how many observations each row represents.

At the end of the report a break summarizes the statistics and computed variables in the report and assigns the value of **TOTALS:** to SECTOR.

The following statements produce Output 5.2:

```
options pageno=1 linesize=72 pagesize=60 nodate fmtsearch=(sasuser);
proc report data=sasuser.grocery headline headskip;
   column sector dept sales profit n;
   define sector / group format=$sctrfmt.;
   define dept   / group format=$deptfmt.;
   define sales  / analysis sum format=dollar9.2;
   define profit / computed format=dollar9.2;

   compute profit;
      if dept='np1' or dept='np2' then profit=0.4*sales.sum;
      else profit=0.25*sales.sum;
   endcomp;

   rbreak after / dol dul summarize;
   compute after;
      sector='TOTALS:';
   endcomp;

   where sector contains 'n';
run;
```

**Output 5.2**
*Report with Groups and a Report Summary*

```
                              The SAS System                              1

        SECTOR     DEPT         SALES       PROFIT         N
        -------------------------------------------------------

        Northeast  Canned      $840.00     $336.00         2
                   Meat/Dairy  $490.00     $122.50         2
                   Paper       $290.00     $116.00         2
                   Produce     $211.00      $52.75         2
        Northwest  Canned    $1,070.00     $428.00         3
                   Meat/Dairy $1,055.00    $263.75         3
                   Paper       $150.00      $60.00         3
                   Produce     $179.00      $44.75         3
        =========             =========   =========  =========
        TOTALS:             $4,285.00    $1,071.25        20
        =========             =========   =========  =========
```

A description of how PROC REPORT builds this report follows:

1. PROC REPORT starts building the report by consolidating the data (SECTOR and DEPT are group variables) and calculating the statistics (SALES.SUM and N) for each detail row and for the break at the end of the report. It stores these values in a temporary file.

2. Now, PROC REPORT is ready to start building the first row of the report. This report does not contain a break at the beginning of the report or a break before any groups, so the first row of the report is a detail row. The procedure initializes all report variables to missing, as Figure 5.1 illustrates. Missing values for a character variable are represented by a blank, and missing values for a numeric variable are represented by a period.

**Figure 5.1**
*Initializing Values for the First Detail Row*

| SECTOR | DEPT | SALES | PROFIT | N |
|--------|------|-------|--------|---|
|        |      | .     | .      | . . |

3. Figure 5.2 illustrates the construction of the first three columns of the row. PROC REPORT fills in values for the row from left to right. Values come from the temporary file created at the beginning of the report-building process.

*Figure 5.2*
*Filling in Values from Left to Right*

| SECTOR | DEPT | SALES | PROFIT | N |
|--------|------|-------|--------|---|
| Northeast | . | | . | . |

| SECTOR | DEPT | SALES | PROFIT | N |
|--------|------|-------|--------|---|
| Northeast | Canned | . | . | . |

| SECTOR | DEPT | SALES | PROFIT | N |
|--------|------|-------|--------|---|
| Northeast | Canned | $840.00 | . | . |

4. The next column in the report contains the computed variable PROFIT. When it gets to this column, PROC REPORT executes the statements in the compute block that is attached to PROFIT. Nonperishable items return a profit of 40%; perishable items return a profit of 25%.

```
if dept='np1' or dept='np2' then profit=0.4*sales.sum;
else profit=0.25*sales.sum;
```

The row now looks like Figure 5.3.

▶ *Caution:*  *Postion of Computed Variables*

Because PROC REPORT assigns values to the columns in a row of a report from left to right, a computed variable can depend only on values to its left.

. . . . . . . . . . . . . . . . . . . . . . . . . . . . . . . . . . . . . . . . . . . . . . . .

*Figure 5.3*
*Adding a Computed Variable to the Row*

| SECTOR | DEPT | SALES | PROFIT | N |
|--------|------|-------|--------|---|
| Northeast | Canned | $840.00 | $336.00 | . |

5. Next, PROC REPORT fills in the value for the N statistic. The value comes from the temporary file created at the beginning of the report-building process. Figure 5.4 illustrates the completed row.

*Figure 5.4*
*First Complete Detail Row*

| SECTOR | DEPT | SALES | PROFIT | N |
|---|---|---|---|---|
| Northeast | Canned | $840.00 | $336.00 | 2 |

6. The procedure writes the completed row to the report.
7. PROC REPORT repeats steps 2, 3, 4, 5 and 6 for each detail row in the report.
8. At the break at the end of the report, PROC REPORT constructs the break lines described by the RBREAK statement. These lines include double underlining, double overlining, and a preliminary version of the summary line. The statistics for the summary line were calculated earlier (see step 1). The value for the computed variables is calculated when PROC REPORT reaches the appropriate column, just as it is in detail rows. PROC REPORT uses these values to create the preliminary version of the summary line (see Figure 5.5).

*Figure 5.5*
*Preliminary Summary Line*

| SECTOR | DEPT | SALES | PROFIT | N |
|---|---|---|---|---|
|  |  | $4,285.00 | $1,071.25 | 20 |

9. If no compute block is attached to the break, the preliminary version of the summary line is the same as the final version. However, in this example, a compute block is attached to the break. Therefore, the next thing that PROC REPORT does is execute the statements in that compute block. In this case, the compute block contains one statement:

```
sector='TOTALS:';
```

This statement replaces the value of SECTOR, which in the summary line is missing by default, with the word **TOTALS:**. After PROC REPORT executes the statement, it modifies the summary line to reflect this change to the value of SECTOR. The final version of the summary line appears in Figure 5.6.

*Figure 5.6*
*Final Summary Line*

| SECTOR | DEPT | SALES | PROFIT | N |
|---|---|---|---|---|
| TOTALS: |  | $4,285.00 | $1,071.25 | 20 |

10. Finally, PROC REPORT writes all the break lines—underlining, overlining, and the final summary line—to the report.

## Building a Report that Uses DATA Step Variables

PROC REPORT initializes report variables to missing at the beginning of each row of the report. The value for a DATA step variable is initialized to missing before PROC REPORT begins constructing the rows of the report and remains missing until you specifically assign it a value. PROC REPORT retains the value of a DATA step variable from the execution of one compute block to another.

Because all compute blocks share the current values of all variables, you can initialize DATA step variables at a break at the beginning of the report or at a break before a break variable. This report initializes the DATA step variable SCTRTOT at a break before SECTOR.

▶ *Caution: Timing at Breaks*

PROC REPORT creates a preliminary summary line for a break before it executes the corresponding compute block. If the summary line contains computed variables, the computations are based on the values of the contributing variables in the preliminary summary line. If you want to recalculate computed variables based on values you set in the compute block, you must do so explicitly in the compute block. This report illustrates this technique.

If no compute block is attached to a break, the preliminary summary line becomes the final summary line.

· · · · · · · · · · · · · · · · · · · · · · · · · · · · · · · · · · · · · · · · · · · · ·

The report in Output 5.3 contains five columns:

□ SECTOR and DEPT are group variables

□ SALES is an analysis variable that is used twice in this report: once to calculate the SUM statistic, and once to calculate the PCTSUM statistic.

□ SCTRPCT is a computed variable based on the values of SALES and a DATA step variable, SCTRTOT, which is the total sales for a sector.

At the beginning of the report, a customized report summary tells what the sales for all stores are. At a break before each group of observations for a department, a default summary summarizes the data for that sector. At the end of each group a break inserts a blank line.

The following statements produce Output 5.3.

**Note:** Calculations of the percentages do not multiply their results by 100 because PROC REPORT prints them with the PERCENT. format.

```
options pageno=1 linesize=72 pagesize=60 nodate fmtsearch=(sasuser);
proc report data=sasuser.grocery noheader nowindows;
   column sector dept sales sctrpct sales=salespct;

   define sector   / 'Sector' group format=$sctrfmt.;
   define dept     / group format=$deptfmt.;
   define sales    / analysis sum format=dollar9.2 ;
   define sctrpct  / computed format=percent9.2 ;
   define salespct / pctsum format=percent9.2;

   compute before;
      line ' ';
      line @20 'Total for all stores is ' sales.sum dollar9.2;
      line ' ';
      line @33 'Sum of' @44 'Percent' @55 'Percent of';
      line @10 'Sector' @21 'Department' @33 'Sales' @44 'of Sector'
           @55 'All Stores';
      line @10 55*'=';
      line ' ';
```

```
            endcomp;

            break before sector / summarize ul;
            compute before sector;
                sctrtot=sales.sum;
                sctrpct=sales.sum/sctrtot;
            endcomp;

            compute sctrpct;
                sctrpct=sales.sum/sctrtot;
            endcomp;

            break after sector/skip;
            where sector contains 'n';
        run;
```

*Output 5.3*
*Report with DATA Step Variables*

```
                                 The SAS System                    1


                        Total for all stores is $4,285.00

                               Sum of     Percent    Percent of
               Sector   Department  Sales   of Sector   All Stores
               ==============================================================

               Northeast             $1,831.00   100.00%    42.73%
               ---------             ---------  ---------  ---------
               Northeast  Canned       $840.00    45.88%    19.60%
                          Meat/Dairy   $490.00    26.76%    11.44%
                          Paper        $290.00    15.84%     6.77%
                          Produce      $211.00    11.52%     4.92%

               Northwest            $2,454.00   100.00%    57.27%
               ---------            ---------  ---------  ---------
               Northwest  Canned     $1,070.00    43.60%    24.97%
                          Meat/Dairy $1,055.00    42.99%    24.62%
                          Paper        $150.00     6.11%     3.50%
                          Produce      $179.00     7.29%     4.18%
```

A description of how PROC REPORT builds this report follows:

1. PROC REPORT starts building the report by consolidating the data (SECTOR and DEPT are group variables) and calculating the statistics (SALES.SUM and SALES.PCTSUM) for each detail row, for the break at the beginning of the report, for the breaks before each group, and for the breaks after each group. It stores these values in a temporary file.
2. PROC REPORT initializes the DATA step variable, SCTRTOT, to missing (see Figure 5.7).

*Figure 5.7   Initializing DATA Step Variables*

| | | Report Variables | | | DATA Step Variable |
|---|---|---|---|---|---|
| **SECTOR** | **DEPT** | **SALES.SUM** | **SCTRPCT** | **SALES.PCTSUM** | **SCTRTOT** |
| | | | | | . |

3. Because this PROC REPORT step contains a COMPUTE BEFORE statement, the procedure constructs a preliminary summary line for the break at the beginning of the report. This preliminary summary line contains values for the statistics (SALES.SUM and SALES.PCTSUM) and the computed variable (SCTRPCT).

At this break, SALES.SUM is the sales for all stores, and SALES.PCTSUM is the percentage those sales represent for all stores (100%). PROC REPORT takes the values for these statistics from the temporary file that it created at the beginning of the report-building process.

The value for SCTRPCT comes from executing the statements in the corresponding compute block. Because the value of SCTRTOT is missing, PROC REPORT cannot calculate value for SCTRPCT. Therefore, in the preliminary summary line (which is not printed in this case), this variable also has a missing value (see Figure 5.8).

The statements in the COMPUTE BEFORE block do not alter any variables. Therefore, the final summary line is the same as the preliminary summary line.

**Note:** The COMPUTE BEFORE statement creates a break at the beginning of the report. You do not need to use an RBREAK statement.

***Figure 5.8*** *Preliminary and Final Summary Line for the Break at the Beginning of the Report*

| Report Variables | | | | | DATA Step Variable |
|---|---|---|---|---|---|
| **SECTOR** | **DEPT** | **SALES.SUM** | **SCTRPCT** | **SALES.PCTSUM** | **SCTRTOT** |
| | | $4,285.00 | . | 100.00% | . |

4. Because the program does not include an RBREAK statement with the SUMMARIZE option, PROC REPORT does not write the final summary line to the report. Instead, it uses LINE statements to write a customized summary that embeds the value of SALES.SUM into a sentence and to write customized column headers. (The NOHEADER option in the PROC REPORT statement suppresses the default column headers, which would have appeared before the customized summary.)

5. Next, PROC REPORT constructs a preliminary summary line for the break before the first group of observations. (This break both uses the SUMMARIZE option in the BREAK statement and has a compute block attached to it. Either of these conditions generates a summary line.) The preliminary summary line contains values for the break variable (SECTOR), the statistics (SALES.SUM and SALES.PCTSUM), and the computed variable (SCTRPCT). At this break, SALES.SUM is the sales for one sector (the **Northeast** sector). PROC REPORT takes the values for SECTOR, SALES.SUM, and SALES.PCTSUM from the temporary file that it created at the beginning of the report-building process.

The value for SCTRPCT comes from executing the statements in the corresponding compute blocks. Because the value of SCTRTOT is still missing, PROC REPORT cannot calculate a value for SCTRPCT. Therefore, in the preliminary summary line, SCTRPCT has a missing value (see Figure 5.9).

***Figure 5.9*** *Preliminary Summary Line for the Break before the First Group of Observations*

| | Report Variables | | | | DATA Step Variable |
|---|---|---|---|---|---|
| SECTOR | DEPT | SALES.SUM | SCTRPCT | SALES.PCTSUM | SCTRTOT |
| Northeast | | $1,831.00 | . | 42.73% | . |

6. PROC REPORT creates the final version of the summary line by executing the statements in the COMPUTE BEFORE SECTOR compute block. These statements execute once each time the value of SECTOR changes.

   □ The first statement assigns the value of SALES.SUM, which in that part of the report represents total sales for one SECTOR, to the variable SCTRTOT.

   □ The second statement completes the summary line by recalculating SCTRPCT from the new value of SCTRTOT. Figure 5.10 shows the final summary line.

▶ ***Caution:*** *Recalculating Values in the Final Summary Line*     If you do not recalculate the value for SCTRPCT, it will be missing because the value of SCTRTOT is missing at the time that the COMPUTE SCTRPCT block executes.

· · · · · · · · · · · · · · ,    · · · · · · · · · · · · · · ·

***Figure 5.10*** *Final Summary Line for the Break before the First Group of Observations*

| | Report Variables | | | | DATA Step Variable |
|---|---|---|---|---|---|
| SECTOR | DEPT | SALES.SUM | SCTRPCT | SALES.PCTSUM | SCTRTOT |
| Northeast | | $1,831.00 | 100.00% | 42.73% | $1,831.00 |

7. Because the program contains a BREAK BEFORE statement with the SUMMARIZE option, PROC REPORT writes the final summary line to the report. The UL option in the BREAK statement underlines the summary line.

8. Now, PROC REPORT is ready to start building the first detail row of the report. It initializes all report variables to missing. Values for DATA step variables do not change. Figure 5.11 illustrates the first detail row at this point.

***Figure 5.11*** *Initializing Values for the First Detail Row*

| | Report Variables | | | | DATA Step Variable |
|---|---|---|---|---|---|
| SECTOR | DEPT | SALES.SUM | SCTRPCT | SALES.PCTSUM | SCTRTOT |
| | | . | . | . | $1,831.00 |

9. Figure 5.12 illustrates the construction of the first three columns of the row.

PROC REPORT fills in values for the row from
from the temporary file it created at the begin

*Figure 5.12*    *Filling in Values from Left to Right*

**Report Variables**

| SECTOR | DEPT | SALES.SUM | SCTRPCT | SALES.PCTSUM | S. |
|--------|------|-----------|---------|--------------|-----|
| Northeast | | . | . | . | $1,831.0 |

| | **Report Variables** | | | | **DATA Step Variable** |
|--------|------|-----------|---------|--------------|-----|
| SECTOR | DEPT | SALES.SUM | SCTRPCT | SALES.PCTSUM | SCTRTOT |
| Northeast | Canned | . | . | . | $1,831.00 |

| | **Report Variables** | | | | **DATA Step Variable** |
|--------|------|-----------|---------|--------------|-----|
| SECTOR | DEPT | SALES.SUM | SCTRPCT | SALES.PCTSUM | SCTRTOT |
| Northeast | Canned | $840.00 | . | . | $1,831.00 |

10. The next column in the report contains the computed variable SCTRPCT. When it gets to this column, PROC REPORT executes the statement in the compute block attached to SCTRPCT. This statement calculates the percentage of the sector's total sales that this department accounts for:

```
sctrpct=sales.sum/sctrtot;
```

The row now looks like Figure 5.13.

*Figure 5.13*    *Adding the First Computed Variable to the Row*

| | **Report Variables** | | | | **DATA Step Variable** |
|--------|------|-----------|---------|--------------|-----|
| SECTOR | DEPT | SALES.SUM | SCTRPCT | SALES.PCTSUM | SCTRTOT |
| Northeast | Canned | $840.00 | 45.88% | . | $1,831.00 |

11. The next column in the report contains the statistic SALES.PCTSUM. PROC REPORT gets this value from the temporary file. The first detail row is now complete (see Figure 5.14).

*First Complete Detail Row*

| | | Report Variables | | | DATA Step Variable |
|---|---|---|---|---|---|
| SECTOR | DEPT | SALES.SUM | SCTRPCT | SALES.PCTSUM | SCTRTOT |
| Northeast | Canned | $840.00 | 45.88% | 19.60% | $1,831.00 |

12. PROC REPORT writes the detail row to the report. It repeats steps 8, 9, 10, 11, and 12 for each detail row in the group

13. After writing the last detail row in the group to the report, PROC REPORT constructs the default group summary. Because no compute block is attached to this break and because the BREAK AFTER statement does not include the SUMMARIZE option, PROC REPORT does not construct a summary line. The only action at this break is that the SKIP option in the BREAK AFTER statement writes a blank line after the last detail row of the group.

14. Now the value of the break variable changes from **Northeast** to **Northwest**. PROC REPORT constructs a preliminary summary line for the break before this group of observations. As at the beginning of any row, PROC REPORT initializes all report variables to missing but retains the value of the DATA step variable. Next, it completes the preliminary summary line with the appropriate values for the break variable (SECTOR), the statistics (SALES.SUM and SALES.PCTSUM), and the computed variable (SCTRPCT). At this break, SALES.SUM is the sales for the Northwest sector. Because the COMPUTE BEFORE SECTOR block has not yet executed, the value of SCTRTOT is still $1,831.00, the value for the Northeast sector. Thus, the value that PROC REPORT calculates for SCTRPCT in this preliminary summary line is incorrect (see Figure 5.15). The statements in the compute block for this break calculate the correct value (see the following step).

**Figure 5.15**  *Preliminary Summary Line for the Break before the Second Group of Observations*

| | | Report Variables | | | DATA Step Variable |
|---|---|---|---|---|---|
| SECTOR | DEPT | SALES.SUM | SCTRPCT | SALES.PCTSUM | SCTRTOT |
| Northwest | | $2,454.00 | 134.00% | 57.27% | $1,831.00 |

▶ *Caution:* *Synchronizing Values for Computed Variables in Break Lines*

If the PROC REPORT step does not recalculate SCTRPCT in the compute block attached to the break, the value in the final summary line will not be synchronized with the other values in the summary line, and the report will be incorrect.

15. PROC REPORT creates the final version of the summary line by executing the statements in the COMPUTE BEFORE SECTOR compute block. These statements execute once each time the value of SECTOR changes.

□ The first statement assigns the value of SALES.SUM, which in that part of the report represents sales for the Northwest sector, to the variable SCTRTOT.

□ The second statement completes the summary line by recalculating SCTRPCT from the new, appropriate value of SCTRTOT. Figure 5.16 shows the final summary line.

*Figure 5.16*    *Final Summary Line for the Break before the Second Group of Observations*

| | Report Variables | | | | DATA Step Variable |
|---|---|---|---|---|---|
| **SECTOR** | **DEPT** | **SALES.SUM** | **SCTRPCT** | **SALES.PCTSUM** | **SCTRTOT** |
| Northwest | | $2,454.00 | 100.00% | 57.27% | $2,454.00 |

Because the program contains a BREAK BEFORE statement with the SUMMARIZE option, PROC REPORT writes the final summary line to the report. The UL option in the BREAK statement underlines the summary line.

16. Now, PROC REPORT is ready to start building the first row for this group of observations. It repeats steps 8 through 16 until it has processed all observations in the input data set (stopping with step 14 for the last group of observations).

# Index

## A

ACROSS option, DEFINE statement  38
across variables  7
  changing default order  7
  defining items as  38
  example  59
  ordering values  41
  reversing display order  39
AFTER location, COMPUTE statement  35
Alias= attribute, DEFINITION window  87
aliases  34–35, 52–53
ANALYSIS option, DEFINE statement  38
analysis variables  7–8
  associating statistics with  7–8, 42
  defining items as  38
  examples  56, 61
  in detail reports  8
  in summary lines  8
  in summary reports  8
  weighting values  48
attributes, setting values  32–33

## B

BEFORE location, COMPUTE statement  35–36
blank lines
  after break lines  46
  beneath column headers  22
  for break lines  30
  in column headers  58
blink attribute  33
BOX option, PROC REPORT statement  21
  example  73
BOX option, ROPTIONS window  98
break lines  14
  colors for  29, 45
  customizing  35, 44, 47
  customizing summaries  14
  default summaries  14
  including summary line as  46–47
  order of  14, 31, 47
  writing blank lines after  46
  writing blank lines for  30
  writing summary line in each group of  30–31
BREAK statement  28–31
  COLOR= option  29
  default summaries  14
  DOL option  29
  DUL option  29
  examples  56, 59
  OL option  29, 56
  options  29–31
  order of break lines  31
  PAGE option  30
  required arguments  28
  SKIP option  30
  SKIP option, examples  56, 59, 64
  SUMMARIZE option  30–31, 56
  SUPPRESS option  31, 56
  syntax  28
  UL option  31

break variables  36
  suppressing  31
BREAK window  78–81
  color list  81
  creating breaks before or after detail rows  78
  default summaries  14
  Double overline summary option  79
  Double underline summary option  79
  Overline summary option  79
  Page after break option  79
  pushbuttons  81
  Skip line after break option  79
  Summarize analysis columns option  80
  Suppress break value option  80
  Underline summary option  79
_BREAK_ variable  24
breaks  14
  creating in BREAK window  78
BY statement  32

## C

CALL DEFINE statement  12, 32–33
CBT entries  22, 40
center justification  21, 38, 97
CENTER option
  DEFINE statement  38
  PROC REPORT statement  21
  ROPTIONS window  97
CHART procedure  74–75
_COL_ automatic variable  32
color attribute  33
COLOR= option
  BREAK statement  29
  DEFINE statement  38
  RBREAK statement  45, 47
colors
  for break lines  29, 45
  for column headers  38
  list in BREAK window  81
  list in DEFINITION window  88
column headers
  breaking  27
  color selection  38
  defining  38–39, 51
  examples  59, 69
  spanning multiple columns  34
  split character  27, 58
  suppressing  24
  underlining  22, 39
  wrapping  28
  writing blank lines beneath  22
  writing blank lines in  58
COLUMN statement  33–35
  examples  58, 61, 69
  report layout  5–6
  required arguments  34–35
  syntax  33
column width  21–22
  example  69
  stacked items  43
column-header option, DEFINE statement  38–39

columns 5–6
  changing default order  7
  defining width  43
  displaying  27
  shared items  8–9
  specifying number of blank characters between  27, 42
  stand-alone items  10
  wrapping  24
Colwidth attribute, ROPTIONS window  99
COLWIDTH= option, PROC REPORT statement  21–22, 51
command attribute  33
COMMAND command  22
command lines, displaying  22
COMMAND option, PROC REPORT statement  22
compound names  12–13, 104–105
compute blocks  11–13
  aliases for report items  34–35
  COMPUTE statement  11, 35–36
  contents  12
  ending  43
  examples  59, 67, 70
  LINE statement  12
  location of execution  35–36
  processing  13
  purpose  11
  referencing report items  12–13
  referencing variables in  12–13
COMPUTE statement  35–36
  AFTER location  35
  BEFORE location  35–36
  compute blocks  11
  examples  54, 69
COMPUTE window  81
COMPUTED option, DEFINE statement  39
COMPUTED VAR window  81–82
  adding computed variables to reports  8, 39
computed variables
  adding to reports  8, 39, 81–82
  examples  59, 66, 69, 74–75
  position of  36
conditional statements, example  67
CSS statistic  11
customized summaries  14, 44–45
  adding from LAYOUT window  92–93
  deleting in LAYOUT window  92–93
customizing break lines  35, 44, 47
CV statistic  11


**D**

DATA COLUMNS window  82
DATA= option, PROC REPORT statement  22
  example  73
DATA SELECTION window  83
DATA step variables  109–115
Data type= attribute, DEFINITION window  87
dates in reports  8
default summaries  14
  adding from LAYOUT window  92
  altering from LAYOUT window  92
  at break  28
  deleting from LAYOUT window  92
  examples  51, 56, 59
  RBREAK statement  14, 45
DEFER mode, ROPTIONS window  97
DEFINE statement  37–43
  ACROSS option  38
  aliases for report items  34–35

ANALYSIS option  38
CENTER option  38
COLOR= option  38
column-header option  38–39
COMPUTED option  39
DESCENDING option  6, 7, 39
DISPLAY option  39
FLOW option  39, 69
FORMAT= option  40
GROUP option  40
ID option  40, 61
ITEMHELP= option  40
LEFT option  40
NOPRINT option  41, 53
NOPRINT option, examples  66, 73
NOZERO option  41
options  38–43
ORDER= option  6, 7, 41, 53
ORDER option  41, 53
overriding options  27
PAGE option  41
report layout  6
required arguments  37
RIGHT option  42
SPACING= option  42
statistic option  42
syntax  37
usages for variables  6
WIDTH= option  43
DEFINITION window  83–88
  Alias= attribute  87
  attributes  84–87
  changing default order of across variables  7
  color list  88
  Data type= attribute  87
  DESCENDING option  87
  FLOW option  87
  ID column option  87
  Item Help= attribute  85
  Justify= attribute  86
  NOPRINT option  87
  NOZERO option  87
  Order= attribute  86
  PAGE option  87
  pushbuttons  88
  Spacing= attribute  85
  specifying usage for variables  6
  Statistic= attribute  85–86
  usage types  84
  Width= attribute  85
DESCENDING option
  DEFINE statement  6, 7, 39
  DEFINITION window  87
detail reports  1
  analysis variables in  8
detail rows  1
  changing default order  6, 7
  creating breaks before or after  78
DISPLAY option, DEFINE statement  39
DISPLAY PAGE window  88
display variables  6, 39
DMS system option  28
DOL option
  BREAK statement  29
  RBREAK statement  46, 51
Double overline summary option, BREAK window  79
double overlining  29, 46, 79
Double underline summary option, BREAK window  79
double underlining  29, 46, 79

double-spaced reports 59
DUL option
   BREAK statement 29
   RBREAK statement 46

# E

ENDCOMP statement 35, 43
   example 54
examples 48–75
EXPLORE window 88–89

# F

FLOW option, DEFINE statement 39
   example 69
FLOW option, DEFINITION window 87
FMTSEARCH= system option 50
form characters 16–17
   changing 17
   default 17
format attribute 33
Format= attribute, DEFINITION window 84–85
FORMAT= option, DEFINE statement 40
FORMAT procedure 49
FORMAT statement 40, 50
formats 40
   examples 54, 69
FORMCHAR= system option 17
   example 63–64
FORMNAME command 15
forms, printing reports with 15
FREE command 15
FREQ statement 43
FSREPORT command 1

# G

GROUP option, DEFINE statement 40
group variables 7
   defining items as 40
   display order 39
   example 56
   ordering values 41
groups
   creating 7
   report building with 105–108

# H

headers
   See column headers
   See page headers
HEADLINE option
   PROC REPORT statement 22, 51
   ROPTIONS window 98
HEADSKIP option
   PROC REPORT statement 22, 51
   ROPTIONS window 98
HELP entries 22, 40
HELP= option, PROC REPORT statement 22
HELP system 1
highlight attribute 33

# I

ID column option, DEFINITION window 87
ID option, DEFINE statement 40
   example 61
ID variables 40
Item Help= attribute, DEFINITION window 85
ITEMHELP= option, DEFINE statement 40

# J

Justify= attribute, DEFINITION window 86

# L

LAYOUT window 90–94
   adding customized summaries 92–93
   adding default summaries 92
   adding report items 91–92
   altering default summaries 92
   altering layout of existing report items 91
   changing report item definitions 91
   changing settings in ROPTIONS window 93–94
   deleting customized summaries 92–93
   deleting default summaries 92
   deleting report items 91–92
   limiting number of observations displayed 94
   navigating 90–91
left justification 21, 40
LEFT option, DEFINE statement 40
LENGTH statement 67
LINE statement 44–45
   compute blocks 12
   examples 54, 67–68
linedrawing 17, 21
Linesize attribute, ROPTIONS window 99
linesize specifications 23, 60, 99
LIST option, PROC REPORT statement 23
LOAD REPORT window 16, 94
LS= option, PROC REPORT statement 23
   example 60

# M

MAX statistic 11, 53
MEAN statistic 10
menu bars, displaying 22
MESSAGE window 95
MIN statistic 11, 53
MISSING option, PROC REPORT statement 10, 23
   example 71
MISSING option, ROPTIONS window 99
missing values
   example 70–71
   in summary lines 30
   MISSING option, PROC REPORT statement 23
   referencing variables with 13

# N

N statistic 10
NAMED option, PROC REPORT statement 24
   example 62
NAMED option, ROPTIONS window 98
new page specification 30, 41, 46

NMISS statistic 10
NOCENTER option, PROC REPORT statement 21
NOEXEC option, PROC REPORT statement 24
NOHEADER option, PROC REPORT statement 24
  example 66
NOHEADER option, ROPTIONS window 98
nonwindowing environment
  REPORT procedure 1, 27–28
NOPRINT option, DEFINE statement 41, 53
  examples 66, 73
NOPRINT option, DEFINITION window 87
NOWINDOWS option, PROC REPORT statement 27–28
NOZERO option
  DEFINE statement 41
  DEFINITION window 87

## O

observations, limiting number displayed 94
OL option, BREAK statement 29
  example 56
OL option, RBREAK statement 46
Order= attribute, DEFINITION window 86
ORDER= option, DEFINE statement 41
  changing default order of variables 6, 7
  example 53
ORDER option, DEFINE statement 41, 53
order variables 6
  defining report item as 41
  display order 39
  ordering values 41
OUT= option, PROC REPORT statement 24, 75
  example 73
output data set
  examples 72–75
  REPORT DATA window 97
  variables in 24
OUTPUT window, printing from 15
OUTREPT= option, PROC REPORT statement 16, 25
  example 62
Overline summary option, BREAK window 79
overlining 29, 46
  suppressing 31

## P

Page after break option, BREAK window 79
page breaks 30, 41, 46
page headers 66, 67
PAGE option
  BREAK statement 30
  DEFINE statement 41
  DEFINITION window 87
  RBREAK statement 46
page size specifications 26, 60, 99
Pagesize attribute, ROPTIONS window 99
PAGESIZE= system option 26
panels 25
  example 63–64
  specifying blank characters between 26
  specifying from ROPTIONS window 100
  specifying number of 25
PANELS= attribute, ROPTIONS window 100
PANELS= option, PROC REPORT statement 25
  example 64

PCTN statistic 11
PCTSUM statistic 11
  example 69
PMENU command 22
pointer controls 44
PRINT command 15
print file, freeing 15
PRINT PAGE command 15
printing reports 15–16
  batch mode 15
  from OUTPUT window 15
  from REPORT window 15
  interactive line mode 16
  noninteractive mode 15
  with forms 15
  with PRINTTO procedure 16
PRINTTO procedure 16
PROC REPORT statement 20–28
  BOX option 21, 73
  CENTER option 21
  COLWIDTH= option 21, 22, 51
  COMMAND option 22
  DATA= option 22, 73
  HEADLINE option 22, 51
  HEADSKIP option 22, 51
  HELP= option 22
  LIST option 23
  LS= option 23, 60
  MISSING option 10, 23, 71
  NAMED option 24, 62
  NOCENTER option 21
  NOEXEC option 24
  NOHEADER option 24, 66
  NOWINDOWS option 27–28
  options 21–28
  OUT= option 24, 73, 75
  OUTREPT= option 16, 25, 62
  PANELS= option 25, 64
  PROFILE= option 25–26
  PROMPT option 26
  PS= option 26, 60
  PSPACE= option 26
  REPORT= option 16, 27, 63
  SHOWALL option 27
  SPACING= option 27, 51
  SPLIT= option 27, 51, 58
  syntax 20
  VARDEF= option 27
  WHERE= option 73
  WINDOWS option 27–28
  WRAP option 28, 62
PROFILE= option, PROC REPORT statement 25–26
PROFILE window 26, 95
profiles 26, 95
PROMPT facility 26
PROMPT mode, ROPTIONS window 97
PROMPT option, PROC REPORT statement 26
PROMPTER window 96
PRT statistic 11
PRTFILE command 15
PS= option, PROC REPORT statement 26
  example 60
PSPACE= attribute, ROPTIONS window 100–101
PSPACE= option, PROC REPORT statement 26
PUT statement 44–45

# R

RANGE statistic 11
RBREAK statement 45–47
COLOR= option 45, 47
default summaries 14, 45
DOL option 46, 51
DUL option 46
OL option 46
options 45–47
order of break lines 47
PAGE option 46
required arguments 45
SKIP option 46
SUMMARIZE option 46–47, 51
syntax 45
UL option 47
windowing environment 47
with BY processing 32
report building 103–115
compound names 104–105
sequence of events 103–104
with DATA step variables 109–115
with groups and report summary 105–108
REPORT DATA window 97
report definitions
creating reports from 16
displaying listing of 24
example 61–63
loading 16, 83, 94
re-using 16
specifying 27
storing 16, 24, 25, 101
titles in 68
writing for use in windowing environment 32
report items 36
adding from LAYOUT window 91–92
aliases for 34–35
altering layout from LAYOUT window 91
calculating value of 47
changing definitions from LAYOUT window 91
defining 6, 83
defining as across variable 38
defining as analysis variable 38
defining as group variable 40
defining as order variable 41
deleting with LAYOUT window 91–92
length 36
referencing in compute blocks 12–13
suppressing 41
type specification 36
report layout 5–11
changing settings 93–94
COLUMN statement 5–6
columns 5–6
DEFINE statement 6
defining items 6
interactions of position and usage 8
statistics 10–11
variables 6–8
REPORT= option, PROC REPORT statement 16, 27
example 63
REPORT procedure
See also BREAK statement
See also COLUMN statement
See also COMPUTE statement
See also DEFINE statement
See also LINE statement
See also PROC REPORT statement

See also RBREAK statement
building reports 103–115
BY statement 32
CALL DEFINE statement 32–33
ENDCOMP statement 35, 43, 54
FREQ statement 43
methods of using 1
nonwindowing environment 1, 27–28
sample reports 1–4
syntax 19–20
WEIGHT statement 48
windowing environment 27–28
windowing environment with prompting facility 1
windowing environment without prompting facility 1
REPORT window 96
printing from 15
reports
changing layout settings 93–94
creating from report definitions 16
customized summary report 4
detail reports 1, 8
double-spaced 59
experimenting with data 88–89
ordered detail report 2
printing 15–16
sample 1–4
SAS dates in 8
summary reports 3, 55–57, 68
unordered detail report 2
right justification 42
RIGHT option, DEFINE statement 42
ROPTIONS window 97–101
attributes 99–101
BOX option 98
CENTER option 97
changing settings 93–94
Colwidth attribute 99
DEFER mode 97
HEADLINE option 98
HEADSKIP option 98
Linesize attribute 99
MISSING option 99
NAMED option 98
NOHEADER option 98
Pagesize attribute 99
PANELS= attribute 100
PROMPT mode 97
PSPACE= attribute 100–101
pushbuttons 101
SHOWALL option 98
SPACING= attribute 100
SPLIT= attribute 100
User Help attribute 101
WRAP option 98
rows
See detail rows
RSTORE window 101
rvsvideo attribute 33

# S

SAS dates 8
SAS log, writing to 23
SHOWALL option
PROC REPORT statement 27
ROPTIONS window 98
Skip line after break option, BREAK window 79

SKIP option, BREAK statement  30
  examples  56, 59, 64
SKIP option, RBREAK statement  46
Spacing= attribute, DEFINITION window  85
SPACING= attribute, ROPTIONS window  100
SPACING= option
  DEFINE statement  42
  PROC REPORT statement  27, 51
SPLIT= attribute, ROPTIONS window  100
split character  27
  example  58
SPLIT= option, PROC REPORT statement  27, 51
  example  58
stacked items  8-9, 34
  column width  43
Statistic= attribute, DEFINITION window  85-86
statistic option, DEFINE statement  42
STATISTIC window  101
statistics  10-11, 101
  associating with analysis variables  7-8, 42
    example  69
STD statistic  10
STDERR statistic  11
storing report definitions  16, 24, 25
SUM statistic  7, 11, 53
  example  69
summaries
  See also default summaries
  customizing  14, 44-45, 92-93
  report building with  105-108
Summarize analysis columns option, BREAK window  80
SUMMARIZE option, BREAK statement  30-31
  example  56
SUMMARIZE option, RBREAK statement  46-47, 51
summary lines  1
  analysis variables in  8
  calculating value of items  30
  including as break lines  46-47
  missing values in  30
  writing in group of break lines  30-31
summary reports  1, 3
  analysis variables in  8
  example  55-57, 68
summary rows  56
SUMWGT statistic  11
Suppress break value option, BREAK window  80
SUPPRESS option, BREAK statement  31
  example  56
suppressing
  break variables  31
  column headers  24
  overlining  31
  report items  41
  titles, in report definitions  68
  underlining  31
SYSDATE automatic macro  50

**T**

T statistic  11
TITLE statement  68

**U**

UL option
  BREAK statement  31
  RBREAK statement  47

Underline summary option, BREAK window  79
underlining  29, 31, 46, 47
  column headers  22, 39
  example  56
  suppressing  31
User Help attribute, ROPTIONS window  101
USS statistic  11

**V**

VAR statistic  11
VARDEF= option, PROC REPORT statement  27
variables
  See also across variables
  See also analysis variables
  See also computed variables
  See also group variables
  See also order variables
  adding to report  82
  aliases for  82-83
  break variables  31, 36
  _BREAK_  24
  changing default order with ORDER= option  6-7
  _COL_  32
  DATA step variables  109-115
  display variables  6, 39
  ID variables  40
  in output data set  24
  interactions of position and usage  8-10
  listing  82
  referencing in compute blocks  12-13
  referencing with missing values  13
  report layout  6-8
  usage  6-8, 84
variances, divisor for  27

**W**

WEIGHT statement  48
WHERE= option, PROC REPORT statement  73
WHERE processing, example  72-73
WHERE statement  50
Width= attribute, DEFINITION window  85
WIDTH= option, DEFINE statement  43
windowing environment
  RBREAK statement  47
  REPORT procedure  27-28
  REPORT procedure with prompting facility  1
  REPORT procedure without prompting facility  1
  writing report definitions for  32
windows
  BREAK  78-81
  COMPUTE  81
  COMPUTED VAR  8, 39, 81-82
  DATA COLUMNS  82
  DATA SELECTION  83
  DEFINITION  83-88
  DISPLAY PAGE  88
  EXPLORE  88-89
  LAYOUT  90-94
  LOAD REPORT  16, 94
  MESSAGE  95
  OUTPUT  15
  PROFILE  26, 95
  PROMPTER  96
  REPORT  15, 96
  REPORT DATA  97

ROPTIONS 97–101
RSTORE 101
STATISTIC 101
WINDOWS option, PROC REPORT statement 27–28
WRAP option, PROC REPORT statement 28
  example 62
WRAP option, ROPTIONS window 98
wrapping
  column headers 28
  columns 24
  examples 62, 69
  FLOW option, DEFINE statement 39
  WRAP option, ROPTIONS window 98

# Your Turn

If you have comments or suggestions about *SAS® Guide to the REPORT Procedure: Reference, Release 6.11,* please send them to us on a photocopy of this page or send us electronic mail.

For comments about this book, please return the photocopy to

> SAS Institute Inc.
> Publications Division
> SAS Campus Drive
> Cary, NC 27513
> **email:** yourturn@unx.sas.com

For suggestions about the software, please return the photocopy to

> SAS Institute Inc.
> Technical Support Division
> SAS Campus Drive
> Cary, NC 27513
> **email:** suggest@unx.sas.com